Discovery Selling®

Discovery Selling®

The Roadmap To Sales Success

By

David Simons
Ginny Simons
Amy Simons, M. Ed.

Discovery Selling® is a registered trademark and service mark of The Performance Resource Group, 6660 S. Sheridan Rd, Suite 120, Tulsa, OK 74133, registered with the U.S. Patent and Trademark Office.

The publication is designed to provide accurate and authoritative information in regard to the subject matter covered. It is sold with the understanding that neither the author nor the publisher is engaged in rendering legal, accounting, or other professional service. If legal advice or other expert assistance is required, the services of a competent professional person should be sought.

ISBN 0-9728412-0-2

Printed in the United States of America

Dedicated to all of the hard-working committed sales professionals in the world who help make the wheels of business turn.

"MEN ARE BEST CONVINCED BY REASONS THAT THEY THEMSELVES DISCOVER."

...Benjamin Franklin

Preface

Professional selling is a profession which requires skills, that is, doing the right things at the right time with the right people to achieve a mutually beneficial outcome. Realizing that skills are important to a sales professional, vast amounts of time, energy and money are invested in "technique" type training. How to close, how to handle objections, how to build instantaneous relationships, how to do dazzling presentations and a vast array of other "techniques" designed to help you get the order.

But a question must be asked here. If you know all of the best techniques, will that insure your success in selling? Better yet, is the best-trained salesperson always the most successful? Is an under-trained or non-trained salesperson automatically doomed to failure? Obviously, the answer is no. Chances are you've personally witnessed sales superstars who had little or no training. Maybe you've seen the reverse as well…a highly trained individual who couldn't succeed. So the question is, why?

To be the best you can be in professional sales, there is a hierarchy of competencies on which one must work consistently and relentlessly. That hierarchy is shown in Figure 1.

The Personal Sales Development Hierarchy

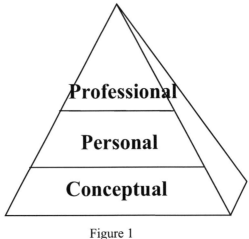

Figure 1

The Discovery Selling® program focuses on all three aspects important to the professional growth and development of a successful seller.

The foundation, as is shown in the Personal Sales Development Hierarchy, is conceptual. In this area, the focus is on one's mindset. What you think about determines what you will do, and in many cases, pre-determines the outcome well in advance of the actual call itself.

Personal issues help deal with those areas which are activity based such as goals, plans, actions, goal measurement systems, interpersonal relationships, communications and personal productivity.

In the professional area of development, you will address your sales process, specific selling skills, gaining commitments, effective prospecting, and building systematic retention processes to retain your clients.

The Discovery Selling® Hierarchy of Qualification

Table of Contents

Table of Contents

3. Relationship

All relationships are based on trust. We'll examine the components of trust utilizing the hierarchy of trust, and then move into the science of NLP (Neuro-Linguistic Programming) where you will discover the modes or ways that people process information, and how to use that information to communicate effectively and powerfully in a way that enhances relationships and fosters understanding.

4. Setting Ground Rules

The Ground Rules formula will give you a simple yet effective means of taking control of the sales call while giving the customer/prospect the ability to feel in control. In this step, you will begin to take control of your process, not of your prospect.

5. From Soaps to Strokes

All human beings are motivated to feel positive and comfortable about themselves, salespeople included. In this session, you'll learn powerful strategies to further bond with your prospect as well as ways to unlock stuck proposals or get calls returned which might be going unanswered now.

6. P.A.I.N./G.A.I.N.

People buy emotionally and justify intellectually. In this step of the selling process, you will discover very specific buying motives. This module will also show you the typical phases, or steps, that individuals as well as organizations go through in the buying process, and offer you some suggestions on aligning yourself with your buyer to enhance the relationship and help you avoid inappropriate or ineffective selling behaviors.

7. Understanding Human Interaction: Key to Effective Communication

This section is right out of the psychology books. Using the sound principles of Dr. Eric Berne and Dr. Tom Harris and their work in Transactional Analysis will help you understand the emotions and thinking processes of both you and your prospects. Choosing how you respond to your prospect's statements will enable you to communicate effectively. Human behavior is predictable. Learn how to predict your prospect's behavior.

8. Questions are The Answer

It is uniformly agreed that listening is one of, if not, the most important professional selling skills. It cannot be underrated. However, unless you know how to ask great questions, the right questions, you may never get a chance to practice that skill. In this section, we'll focus on your questioning skills, and help you learn specific questions to ask to navigate the sales process.

9. The Vision of Solution

In this module, you'll learn how to help your buyer to put "you" in his picture. When you can help your prospect visualize the conceptual framework of your solution, you create a preference in the buyer's mind to your company, your product and to you that will make it difficult for your competitor to overcome.

10. Investment

Money is always an issue, but it is seldom the only issue and rarely the highest priority. By dealing with budget and investment at the appropriate time, you reduce the chances of losing because of price. This will also enable you to have a strong value conversation. Consequently, you will build value in your product, your service and your company.

.11. Decision and Authority

At some point, a decision must be made to move forward with you, or a competitive product, or to do nothing at all. It is important to understand all of the elements of decision-making including the process, the people and the timing, in order to reduce your sell cycle length, and get faster decisions. How individuals make decisions, personally, is critically important for a salesperson to understand. Using the DISC Behavioral Style model, you'll learn about your own decision making style, and how to read the style of others.

12. The Major Contract

The major contract is a summation of all of the activities that have transpired to this point in the sales process. It is at this point that you have a qualified prospect who has earned the right to a proof presentation or demonstration.

13. Proof Presentations

Now is the time to show your stuff. Understand
what a proof presentation, or any presentation,
really is and what you should do in this step to
leave with the order!

14. Retention

Keeping customers once the sale is made is
paramount to on-going success. Learn specific
steps on retaining customers for life. Building a
database of happy satisfied clients will go far in
building your business. Learn how to be the
recipient of a steady stream of testimonials and
referrals.

"In times of change, learners shall inherit the earth, while the learned find themselves beautifully equipped to deal with a world that no longer exists."

Eric Hoffer

The Ordeal of Change

Introduction

Welcome! We're pleased that you have chosen to take part in this innovative and informative sales training program. It is the culmination of many years of work and the effort of hundreds of salespeople and clients from a variety of industries. Each has contributed to its completion.

Selling, as if you have not noticed, is a much different profession today than it has been. Technology has combined with sophistication at the buying level to make much of what we do as salespeople more important than ever. The seller's behavior, when faced with a buyer, is now a more critical component of success than one had ever predicted that it would be.

Several years ago, it was predicted that the Internet would lead to the end of salespeople...that they would go the way of the dinosaur and everyone would rely on this new form of access to companies and products as the means to buying. And, to a certain degree that has come to pass. However, the profession of selling is alive and well, and also more important than ever. What has gone away, or soon will, is the type of salesperson that brings nothing more to the table than a group of techniques and high-pressure tactics. Buyers today will not tolerate it. They don't have to. They have far more choices than ever before...one of them being e-commerce.

If ever there was a time when you, as a salesperson, played a key role in the success of your company's future, that time is now. Selling is not about delivering proposals or quotes, responding to RFP's (Request for Proposal) or competitively bidding. Selling today must be from the customer's perspective or it will be difficult to succeed.

The implications are far-reaching because what it means is that in spite of the predictions of the salesperson becoming obsolete, quite the contrary is true. With a myriad of choices, people need help choosing the solution which is best for them, and they don't know how to do that without help.

The lesson here is that skillful salespeople will excel and prosper, and the bad ones will go away. To prove this point, research conducted by the H. R. Chally Group continues to show that the single most important factor for a buyer when choosing a vendor is the salesperson. Other factors such as quality, full range solutions and delivery are important, but do not overshadow the importance of the salesperson as the primary selection factor. Price continues to remain low on the list.

Selling, then, is a people-to-people profession. Proposals, brochures, slick marketing pieces or premiums don't sell...people do! And that's the heart of this program. While it will help you better understand your products and services, it will truly help you understand your customers. Relating to people and leading them to decisions that are in their best interest is where you will achieve success.

The Discovery Selling® process is not a technique-laden program with a plethora of magical one-liners and snappy comebacks to the most common objections. It is a methodology to help you communicate more deeply, more effectively, and more honestly with every prospective customer that you meet. When people realize that you are working diligently to help them serve their own self-interests, yours become fulfilled as a consequence of that action. It will help you become a valued resource, rather than a mere sales rep or product peddler.

Jack Welch, former Chairman and CEO of GE is quoted as saying, "One thing we've discovered with certainty is that anything we do that makes the customer more successful, inevitably results in a financial return for us." That sentiment sums up the philosophy of the Discovery Selling® process in which you are about to participate.

A warning however; this program will cause you to stretch. It is a paradigm shift from where you might be at the present time. However, know this...it works. It has been tried, field-tested and used by thousands of salespeople in a variety of professions. Each person can use his or her own unique style and personality in its implementation. Your intention that is your reasons behind anything you do, **shout more loudly** that anything you actually do. If you are truly working in the best interest of your customer, he knows it. If you are working just to make a sale, get the quick hit and move on to the next opportunity, he knows that too.

So above all, stay focused on the best interests of your customers and they will respond in kind.

One further point should be made here. There is not one universal, right way to sell, but there are certain universal principles that always apply. There are certain things, steps if you will, that you always take in the process of selling effectively to meet client needs. It is those steps upon which this program is based.

Effective selling is...

- Doing the right things

- Doing them at the right time

- Doing them with the right people

- Doing them for the right reasons, to achieve the right decision.

This sales development and training program is designed to help you do just that.

It is our hope that you will use it and contribute to its growth. It is a dynamic process, much changed from its original design ten years ago, and it will continue to change. Please let us know how we might improve it to make it more effective for both customers and salespeople. It is, after all, designed to make a difference in the lives of all who are impacted by it.

Thanks again for your participation, and our best wishes for your continued success.

The Discovery Selling® Training Team

Definition of Selling

Selling is the art and science of inspiring people to discover that which is in their best interest by helping them get in touch with what's important to them on a personal, emotional level.

On the following page, you will find a list of

mixed up numbers. You have **one minute** to

find and circle the numbers in sequence

(1-100). Turn the page and begin.

97	21	37	9	61	14	74	26	6	94
89	49	1	53	81	34	82	46	66	18
13	57	25	17	65	90	22	70	30	58
77	33	73	45	93	38	78	2	42	86
41	69	85	29	5	98	50	62	54	10
63	7	79	39	15	76	48	12	16	96
75	47	27	59	31	100	24	36	56	68
3	43	23	19	71	4	52	40	32	60
83	11	91	35	87	72	28	80	8	84
55	95	51	99	67	20	88	44	92	64

Can you see the pattern of how the numbers are arranged? They are placed in a "Z" pattern.

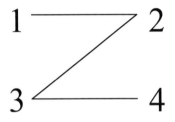

Now repeat the same exercise. You have one minute to circle as many numbers as you can in sequence.

You have one minute to repeat the exercise.

Turn the page and begin.

97	21	37	9	61	14	74	26	6	94
89	49	1	53	81	34	82	46	66	18
13	57	25	17	65	90	22	70	30	58
77	33	73	45	93	38	78	2	42	86
41	69	85	29	5	98	50	62	54	10
63	7	79	39	15	76	48	12	16	96
75	47	27	59	31	100	24	36	56	68
3	43	23	19	71	4	52	40	32	60
83	11	91	35	87	72	28	80	8	84
55	95	51	99	67	20	88	44	92	64

Results

How far did you get the first time?

_____

How far did you get the second time?

_____

% Improvement

☐

What would happen if you could improve your sales results by that percentage? Did you work any harder the second time?

Having a process by which to sell will help you increase your efficiency, close more sales while not working harder…

JUST SMARTER!

What is a Selling System?

A Selling System is an overall strategy and set of tactics designed to ensure that each time you engage in any type of buyer-seller interaction, it is handled in as close to the optimum way as is humanly possible.

Too often Sales People attempt to control the Buyer. The reality is that they should only control their process. By so doing, they *retain control* without *being controlling*, pushy, manipulative or arrogant.

A superior process will give you superior results.

High Performance Selling

The discipline of maximizing the return on the investment of your three primary inventories in each selling opportunity.

Your three primary inventories are:

1) TIME

What ways is your time used?

_____

_____

2) ENERGY

What ways do you use your energy?

_____

_____

3) RESOURCES

What resources do you or your company use with a customer?

_____

_____

High Performance Selling

List 3 ways to maximize your time.

_____

_____

_____

List 3 ways to maximize your energy.

_____

_____

_____

What ways can maximize you and your company's resources?

_____

_____

_____

Primary Selling Skills

Certain skills are necessary during the sales encounter. On the following page you will find a partial list of Primary Selling Skills. Each skill has the first letter in place to help you.

CAN YOU GUESS THE
PRIMARY SELLING
SKILLS?

Primary Selling Skills

Fill in the Blanks.

- L_____

- Q_____

- Q_____

- Dealing with the Buyer's P_____ C_____

- Understanding T_____ B_____ M_____

- D_____ Yourself/Your Company from the C_____

- G_____ C_____

- B_____ R_____

- C_____

- P_____

- D_____ a S_____-M_____ S_____

The Training Goal

The Discovery Selling® is designed to introduce you to a new, systematic way of approaching your sales opportunities. It will lay the groundwork to help you achieve advanced sales mastery.

Primary Selling Skills

Answer Key

How well did you do? Check your answers.

- Listening Skills

- Qualification

- Questioning Skills

- Dealing with the Buyer's Primary Concerns

- Understanding True Buyer's Motives

- Differentiating Yourself/Your Company from the Competition

- Getting Commitment

- Building Relationships

- Communication Skills

- Presentation Skills

- Developing a Self-Motivation System

The Adult Learning Model

The learning process never ends, even when we become adults. There are specific steps that one must go through in the learning process. As adults, we are not as accepting of information that we receive from outside sources. Too often we deny the necessity to change. The precursor to all learning is the Denial Stage. Children do not usually go through this stage because they have not learned to judge new concepts. Children are completely open and accepting of new concepts, whether they are true or not. That is why it is so important to monitor the influence other people have on our children. Adults, however, have learned to use their past experiences to determine if indeed a change in behavior (learning) is warranted. Oftentimes adults will deny the necessity to change. If this is the case, no learning will ever occur.

The first step in the Adult Learning Model is **Awareness**. Before we can learn anything we have to become aware of the performance gap that exists between what we would like to see happen, verses what is actually happening. A great analogy would be taking golf lessons. We only go to a golf instructor after we become aware that something is wrong with our swing and we don't know how to correct it ourselves because we can't determine what we are doing wrong.

The second step is **Knowledge**---Gaining the new information. We go to a golf instructor so he can tell us what we are doing incorrectly and also tell us how to fix it. Oftentimes, the knowledge he gives us is relatively simple, but in the long run makes a big difference on our game.

The third step is **Skill**. In this step it is necessary to put into practice the newly acquired information. This part of the learning model is the most difficult. Using golf again as our example, it is now time to practice using the knowledge we acquired from the instructor. During this stage, we are consciously thinking about what we have to do and we sometimes feel awkward in doing the new behavior. This is the stage that takes the longest time, involves much repetition, and requires tenacity.

The fourth step is **Mastery**. This is also known as Internalization. Once you reach the Mastery stage, your new learning has become second nature. It is part of what you do automatically without have to concentrate. The new behavior no longer feels awkward. True learning has occurred.

These stages occur in any learning situation. Learning is gradual and incremental. Throughout the Discovery Selling® modules you will notice that there is much repetition. The authors are not being redundant. They are following the adult learning model.

The Adult Learning Model

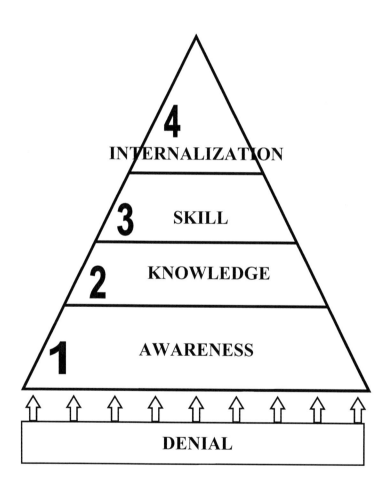

The Behavior Change Model

Training is about behavior change NOT acquired knowledge. Learning new behaviors means change. Human beings resist change. All humans have a natural tendency to remain in the "Comfort Zone". However, if one is to grow, one must accept the fact that it is necessary to move out of the comfort zone and move into the learning zone. Setting goals is necessary for growth. Unfortunately, any goal you aspire to forces you to move out of your Comfort Zone. The definition of a goal is a *planned conflict with the status quo.* It is important to realize you are going to feel conflict when you move into the learning zone. Understanding that learning is gradual and incremental will help you also understand that change initiated rapidly may have an adverse effect. Rapid change may propel you into the Panic Zone. Once in the Panic Zone, human nature will force you to retreat to the Comfort Zone where there is safety. You will revert to your old habits where there is comfort. This is known as Behavioral Elasticity. The goal of Discovery Selling® is to keep you in the Learning Zone.

The Behavior Change Model

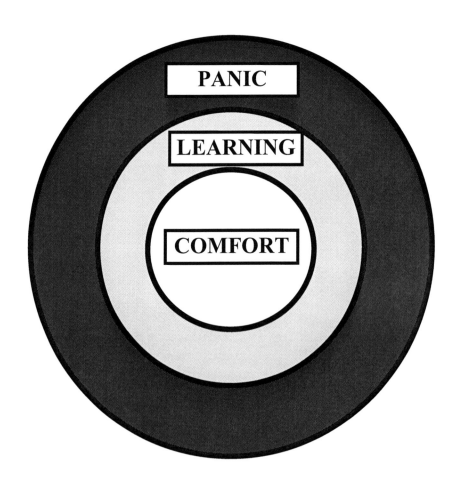

Top Five Selling Difficulties

1. _____

2. _____

3. _____

4. _____

5. _____

How do your difficulties compare to difficult selling situations on the following page?

Difficult Selling Situations

- Hard to differentiate from the competition

- Buyer is well educated about product or service

- Small company selling to large company

- The buyer does not understand the product/service

- Low risk buyer

- Buyer doesn't care

- The user can't buy

- Perceived as expensive

- Requires buyer to make major changes

- Multiple decision-makers

- Heavy competition

- Seldom find buyers who know they need us

- Doesn't believe in your product/service

You are about to embark on a journey into Discovery Selling® that will address the various difficulties you and others face in the exciting profession of SELLING. Fasten your seat belts and ENJOY YOUR TRIP!

The Dance of Deception

The Dance of Deception

Have you ever watched a couple on the dance floor who really seem to go together? They move together in sync and seem to be totally enjoying themselves. When observing them, it's hard to determine which partner is leading and which is following. But as you observe them, you get the sense that it is a beautiful display of perfect harmony.

Conversely, have you ever been dancing with someone who can't lead, or worse yet is supposed to be following and keeps trying to take control of the dance. It is certainly not a beautiful display of harmony, nor is it a pleasant experience, nor do the people seem to be enjoying themselves. If you happen to be the woman, your only thought is to get off the dance floor as soon as possible. If you are the man, your only thought is to get off the dance floor as soon as possible. If you are an observant, you can clearly sense the tension in the air and see disharmony in action.

Selling is very much like a dance. Someone wants to lead the dance. Usually it is the buyer.

The Buyer's Usual Tactics

Most buyers will attempt to take control of the sales process through the following steps:

1. Dance of Deception
   a. Misrepresentation #1(little white lies)
   b. Misrepresentation #2
2. Great Brain Robbery

3. Academy Awards

4. Role Reversal

5. Confuse and Delude

6. Hide and Seek

Let's look at each one of these steps individually to help you understand what's happening in most sales situations.

1. The Dance of Deception

A. Misrepresentation #1— sounds something like, "I really don't need what you sell, but I'll make an appointment with you anyway."

Power Principle:
All human behavior is purposeful.
People don't do things by accident or randomly. When someone agrees to meet with you, it is for a reason. You must discover what that reason is.

Power Principle:
All human behavior has a positive intent.
People will only do that which they perceive to be in their best interest.

As salespeople, we realize that the only way to grow our business is to get in front of people. When prospects position themselves as granting us a favor, we then are psychologically at a disadvantage. Subconsciously, we realize that by getting an appointment we have one less cold call to make; therefore, we place too much importance on the call. We find ourselves hoping that through our expertise (or luck), we might even be able to close the sale. We move ourselves into "Hope and Pray" selling.

Selling is more controlled by your thoughts, beliefs, and emotions than by your skills. If you are feeling "blessed" because someone has agreed to talk to you, and the prospect tells you that you have 15 minutes to sell him, what do you do? You probably go into the salesperson "spew". The prospect may even perceive you as acting a little needy.

Power Principle:
Power buys from power.

If the prospect detects that you *need* the business, not want it, but *need* it, then what happens to his perception of your power? Are you selling on an even keel? Are you at the same social/psychological level as the prospect? I don't think so. To make matters worse, no one wants to do business with a needy salesperson.

    B. Misrepresentation #2- In this instance, the prospect calls you and says he is unhappy with his current supplier. He has heard good things about your company and he would like to talk to you. You, as a salesperson, feel like you hit the mother lode. You have a hot prospect.

Typically, your self-talk on the way to the appointment sounds something like, "I have a hot one. I better not mess it up. I think this one will help me meet quota this month. This is a done deal."

You get into your meeting and the prospect says, "So, tell me what you can do for us. You only have fifteen minutes." What do you do? -- probably "spew". Why? Because, you don't want to lose the sale. Then, after listening to you for fifteen minutes, the prospect blesses you with the opportunity to go back to your office and do a proposal. He is also very complimentary about you and your company. He tells you that everything you have talked about sounds pretty good. It looks like your company might be just the solution that his company needs. The prospect has set you up for step #2.

2. THE GREAT BRAIN ROBBERY

The Great Brain Robbery is where you solve the prospect's problem without getting paid.

You now go back to your office all excited because the prospect was so nice to you. You are even thinking that the prospect and you hit it off pretty well. Your boss asks you how the meeting went and you respond that it went very well and that you have a good chance of getting the order, "It's practically in the bag." But, you reiterate to your boss, that it is imperative that you be priced better than the competition. By the way, the generic name we use for the competition is Horace and Hortense.

You are now deeply involved in the process of expending your three primary inventories: Time, Energy, and Resources. You have already invested time on the appointment. You are getting ready to invest more time to do a proposal. Your energy is equally invested. You are beginning to tap into your company's resources, which include:

- The expertise of key players in your company that have spent years in learning everything there is to know about your product

- The research your company has invested many thousands of dollars to develop

- The administrative help needed to make the proposal top notch.

The misrepresentations or lies the prospect tells are guilt free. Why? Because lies one tells to salespeople don't count. They don't count because everyone has a right to protect himself from danger. Oftentimes, at a subconscious level, prospects view the salesperson as dangerous.

Exercise:

You may recall an old television show called $20,000 Pyramid. It stared Dick Clark. The object of the game was to get your partner to guess the "secret word" by using adjectives. You were not allowed to use any part of the 'secret word' while giving the clues.

Imagine that you are a contestant on the TV game show $20,000 Pyramid. The secret word is 'Salesperson'. If you can get your partner to guess the word before your opponent can get his partner to guess the secret word, you will win $20,000.

Write down the adjectives you would use for 'salesperson'.

_____

_____

_____

Typically, the words that are used, time and time again, are words like: Sleazy, Pushy, Polyester, Snake Oil, Liar, Herb Tarlek, etc.

You might be saying to yourself, "I don't act sleazy, pushy, etc." Why do salespeople have such a bad reputation?

There are salespeople who stretch the truth, are pushy, and don't know when to back off. Please understand, that we are not saying you as a salesperson have these characteristics. What we are saying is that there are salespeople out there who are exhibiting these behaviors daily.

It's fair to say that everyone has had at least one bad experience with a salesperson. It doesn't take too many before one learns how to protect himself from an unpleasant situation. The prospect does it by withholding information and telling misrepresentations. In essence, past negative experiences with salespeople have taught prospects they need to protect themselves.

You have fervently worked on your proposal. You invest several hours to make sure you have all of your "i's" dotted and "t's" crossed. By tapping into your company's resources, you have even been able to develop an innovative solution that not only saves them money, but also saves them manpower. You can't wait to present your proposal. You know that you are going to blow Horace out of the water.

The big day arrives. You are ready. This sale will put you six months ahead of your quota. You have already calculated the commission you will receive and you believe it will be enough to purchase the next toy on your wish list.

3. The Academy Awards

The prospect seems very receptive to your ideas. He starts selling you on the good job you and your company have done. He tells you that your proposal looks very good, and that they are probably going to make a decision in the very near future. He just needs to "run it by" some people. He tells you that it is looking like you have done the best job so far. It's looking like your company and his company are going to have a great future together.

You are feeling like a million bucks. He likes you and he likes what you have shown him. He doesn't even seem blown away by the price. As a matter of fact, he didn't even try to get you to lower the price.

The prospect has just given you an award winning performance. The prospect has just gone through a two-act play.

Act 1---The Strokes--He has made you feel good. He has said some really nice things to you to make you feel *special.*

Power Principle:
If a prospect gives you strokes, he is not giving you money. Strokes are your payment.

Act 2—Weak and Wimpy words---Weak and Wimpy words don't have any real meaning. Words like: probably, near future, looking good, maybe, sometime, possibility, etc. Weak and wimpy words serve two purposes. The first is to offer you some hope so he doesn't make you feel bad for robbing you of your information. The second is to keep you on the hook in case he needs more unpaid consulting by having you revise your proposal.

4. Role Reversal

The prospect is buying time so he can check with Horace. What do you think Horace is going to say when he shows him your proposal? Chances are Horace will say that he can do what you are proposing. He not only can do as your proposal suggests, but he can probably cut the price a little (He is able to make that claim because he did not use his Time, Energy, and Resources).

The prospect sells you the "lie" that you are going to get the business. He gives you some form of "think it over". He needs to check your proposal with Horace. There is a slight chance that Horace may not be able to step up. The prospect has to make sure that he can still use you just in case things don't work out as anticipated. What you should understand at this point, is that you are probably nothing more than negotiating leverage for your prospect.

5. Confuse and Delude

The prospect confuses and deludes you, the salesperson. You leave the call feeling like this is a done deal. He had nothing negative to say. You even go back to your office and tell your boss that you have this one. You are just waiting on some formalities (like the P.O. or the Contract). The boss asks you when the formalities are going to take place. You tell him that the prospect said he would get back to you by the end of the week.

6. Hide and Seek

The end of the week arrives. All day Friday, you expend more energy on waiting for the call. You don't think it would be prudent to leave the office because you may miss the big call. By about 4:30, you decide you will wait fifteen more minutes and then initiate contact. By the time you make the call, the prospect has already left for the day. You go home thinking that hopefully the prospect forgot his promise and that you will touch base with each other on Monday.

Monday arrives. You try to call the prospect and you hear statements like: "He is in a meeting;" "He is out to lunch;" "He is on vacation;" "He is at a funeral;" etc. You now start the fun and games of voice mail.

Power Principle:
When you run into a 'Think It Over', there is only one person thinking it over--- THE SALESPERSON. The minute you walk out of the office, the prospect doesn't think another thought about you or your proposal.

In review, the prospect takes your proposal to Horace. Horace says he can do exactly what your proposal suggests. He could even do it a little cheaper.

Do you get the business or does Horace get the business? Probably Horace. He gets the business because he already has a relationship established.

Between every buyer and seller there is a huge crevice.

Within this crevice is fear and distrust.

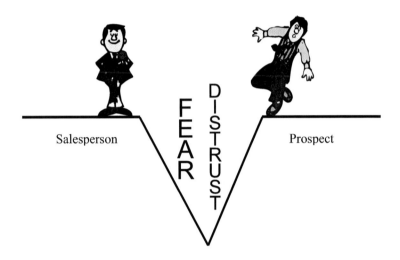

Salesperson | FEAR DISTRUST | Prospect

When we talk about Horace having a relationship, what we are actually saying is that he causes less fear and distrust. Horace has closed the gap.

The Buyer-Seller Dance is a psychological game. Like any game, there is a winner, loser and a set of rules.

Unfortunately, the salesperson becomes the loser, because he is playing by a set of rules of which he is unaware and which are designed to favor the prospect. The salesperson is in the dark, playing a game he can't win.

There is a better way. Selling should be a totally honest interaction, where all parties know what is going on at all times; and either party has the right to end the interaction at any point in time. All sales should have a win/win outcome where there is mutual commitment and comfort to adhere to a set of rules agreed upon by both parties.

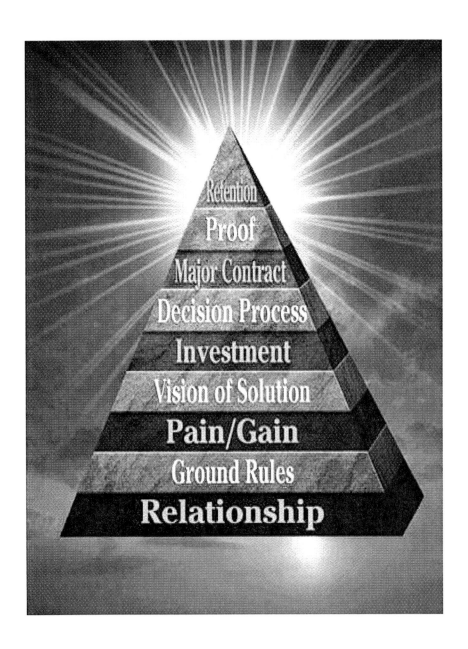

The Qualification Hierarchy

Professional selling is an interesting endeavor. It is a profession that one can enter without years of education; in fact almost anyone who wants to enter into a sales career will usually be given a chance to do so. The price of admission is low, yet the payoff can be extremely high. The price of success in selling, however, is quite a different matter. Like anything in life, it takes little effort to be average and dedicated effort to achieve success.

Many people go into professional selling either because someone told them they "would be good at it" or because that was the only job they could find. Others, much smaller in number, do so because they are dedicated and committed to the profession and choose it as their livelihood. They love to sell, they love their job, and are committed to being "masters of the game". Whatever brought you into this profession, realize that there are right and wrong ways of doing it, just as there are in any profession.

Consider athletics for a moment. Let's use tennis as an example. Almost anyone can play tennis but not everyone can play tennis well. The masters compete at an entirely different level than the masses. Truly great athletes (the names are too numerous to mention) are the ones that dedicate themselves to their chosen endeavor. They approach it with discipline and with dedication and are continually working on improving their performance. They practice relentlessly. Amateurs are usually not able to effectively compete with their professional counterparts, and if they do, they usually wind up defeated. What's the difference? The ability to EXECUTE. Many could, but most won't. They do not have the personal commitment to do what it takes to achieve master level success.

Selling is like any other skill-based activity. Almost anyone can play, but it takes training, discipline, practice and focused dedication to play the game well. And check it out, the truly great performers in any endeavor – be it sports, or medicine or sales - never forget to continually work on the basics! Instead of viewing the basics as routine and boring, the true masters of any human endeavor, professional selling included, see it as essential to their success. If you cannot execute the basics, you are doomed to the life of being a runner-up, because you will never master the advanced concepts.

When you compete against a master seller, you'll know it. They'll beat you every time if you're not ready. The question you must ask yourself is, "Am I ready to play and to win?" The Discovery Selling® training program will prepare you to compete to win through an understanding and mastery of basic processes, as well as, more advanced principles of high sales performance. When you master the basics of the system and discipline yourself to execute that systematic process in every sales encounter, you will see vast improvement in your results.

The Discovery Selling® Process

The Discovery Selling® process is the culmination of years of trial and error, actual in-the-field use and continuous refinement. More than just mere tactics that can, in many cases alienate a prospective buyer, you'll find that Discovery Selling® actually enhances relationships. Much of the material upon which the program has been developed comes from research on psychology, as well as, actual data about the way people buy and make decisions.

Almost everyone who has learned the Discovery Selling® process and implemented it has experienced improvement in their results. It matters not if you're new to the profession or a seasoned pro. The process works every time. So the question is, should you change the way you're currently selling? No one can answer that question but you. However, before you answer, check your results. Could your results be significantly better or are you settling for less than what you can produce? Are you closing less than 50% of your proposals and/or trials? Would you like to increase your income with less effort? Would you like to shorten your sales cycle? Would you like a way to eliminate objections rather than just overcome them? Would you like to forecast future sales with an 85%

accuracy? Would you like to be in total control of your selling at every moment? If you answered yes to these questions then fasten your seat belt and get ready for the Discovery Selling® experience.

Why A Selling Process?

Imagine for a moment that you are standing at the edge of a pond. The surface of the water is as smooth as glass. You have a stone in your hand and throw it into the middle of the pond. Obviously, that stone, when it hits the water, will cause ripples to spread outward in all directions. Even after the stone has sunk to the bottom, the ripples will continue outward in all directions. That stimulus has caused an effect on the surface of the water that lasts long after the event that created it. The stone started a sequence of events that continue into the future.

Likewise, in selling, much of what we do, particularly in the early stages of the selling process, creates a "ripple effect". What we do at the beginning stages has far reaching consequences. If we do the right things early, the events that happen later are far more positive.

The game of chess, as an example, is one of the best metaphors to use for selling. Any chess master will tell you that a player's opening moves, or gambits as they are called, are the most crucial in a match. They will also tell you that almost nothing you do in the later part of the match will compensate for poor opening moves. In essence, what you do at the beginning determines what will happen in the end. The results are pre-determined by your opening strategy.

Like in a game of chess, beginning a sales cycle poorly with a given prospect could mean that you may never recover. Open with strong moves and your outcomes improve in measurable ways. It is this theory upon which the Discovery Selling® process is based. Successful "opening" in professional selling means *effective qualification*.

The concept of qualifying a buyer is one with which every salesperson agrees. Yet when it comes right down to it, they frequently do not truly qualify, based upon their outcomes. If a salesperson truly qualified every prospect and presented only to those who met their qualification minimums, they would close nearly 100% of their proposals and trials. Instead, after the fact, they discover the truth. The truth that would have let them know early on that there was a very limited possibility of doing business.

They were involved in a no-win situation. They invested their precious time, energy and resources on a non-qualified prospect.

Qualification of a buyer is not just important; it is *essential* if you are to manage your precious time effectively and efficiently.

What are some of the indicators that tell you that you have not qualified effectively (if at all)? Here they are:

- Prospect doesn't have the budget or will not invest (You cannot help someone who is unable or unwilling to make the necessary investment of money)

- Prospect is not the decision-maker (You cannot help someone who can't make a decision)

- The prospect never told you his real evaluation criteria or Vision of Solution (You cannot help someone unless you can deliver what he wants)

- The prospect wouldn't share his real needs or P.A.I.N.
  (You cannot help someone who has no real needs)

All of these *mandatory qualification factors* tell you whether or not you had complete information. Information – accurate information – is the key to qualification.

Without it you are forced into a game of guessing.

Power Principle:
NO GUESSING!

The most common indicator of presenting solutions to non-qualified prospects is low closing percentages (usually 25-30% or lower).

It is surprising how many proposals are delivered and the number of trials which are initiated, that are doomed to failure from the start because of insufficient or ineffective qualification. For instance, if you knew in advance that your prospect had a budget problem (the problem being he didn't have one and either couldn't or wouldn't create one) would you still do a trial? NO WAY! So find out. The information is there if you'll commit to finding it. You must find it if you want to win.

Unlike most traditional selling approaches, which are back-loaded, Discovery Selling® is a front-loaded process. Just as in the chess match, it insures that what you do in the beginning will lead to a dramatically improved outcome. Admittedly, you'll have to do more work at the front end of the selling process, but rest assured that it's work you'll have to do anyway. In fact, it's work you are doing presently when you successfully complete a sale. The sooner you cover the qualification factors, the sooner you either eliminate the prospect or move on to consummate the sale.

WARNING!

You must fight your temptation to present your solutions or describe your products until you've qualified the prospect. Why? Because, unless your buyer is qualified he can't or won't buy them anyway, so why bother?

The Discovery Selling® process is a nine-step sequence of selling steps, organized in a manner consistent with the steps that a buyer takes in his buying process. That means, you'll be perfectly aligned with your buyer every time, thus enhancing relationship as well as buyer satisfaction.

THE DISCOVERY SELLING®

QUALIFICATION HIERARCHY

Let's briefly describe the **Qualification Hierarchy**, to give you a general overview of the process, and thus set the stage for your progression through this program.

Relationship

There are no social calls in sales. This being said, Relationship does not mean friendship in the context of effective selling. Rather, Relationship describes the creation of a zone of safety, established by the salesperson that helps the prospect feel comfortable enough to share critical information with you. Without pertinent information from your prospect you cannot sell, you can only "pitch" products.

If the prospect perceives that you are a threat, for whatever reason, he will believe it to be in his best interest to either withhold important information or refuse to answer. He might even mislead you. Your goal in this step is to build a trust relationship so that there can be a productive two-way flow of information between you and your prospect.

Qualification requires accurate and timely information…you cannot qualify without it. In the Relationship Module, you'll discover how to read your prospect, how to begin building a trust relationship from the very first contact, and most importantly you'll discover that some of the things you may have been taught in the past might actually be hurting the relationship rather than enhancing it.

Ground Rules

Setting the Ground Rules helps you take control of the selling process without attempting to manipulate or control the prospect. This all-important step will develop an atmosphere of trust and help you achieve your call objectives.

P.A.I.N./G.A.I.N.

There is one universal thing that all human beings share...we are emotional creatures. Emotions, more than any other factor, govern our behavior. It is impossible for us to act in any other way than emotional because, if we did, we would not be human. The single strongest emotion that causes people to take action is the emotion of pain. When a person is in pain, he will do almost anything to get out of it. Likewise, when someone desperately wants something, the pleasant feelings associated with gaining what he desires will cause a person to take action.

People, all people, make emotional decisions and then justify those decisions intellectually. This means that when we sell, we must appeal to a person's emotions first and their intellect second. In this module, we find out where the prospect hurts and if he wants some help eliminating his P.A.I.N. or achieving his G.A.I.N..

Vision of Solution

Prospects must have a picture – a Vision - of what they want to achieve and of how they want their P.A.I.N. eliminated. You must be in that picture. Furthermore, you must clearly understand that goal or Vision. In this selling step, with the help of your prospect, you'll collaborate to set expectations, design the ideal solution, and build a preference for your company and your solutions.

In this step you will also discover the specific criteria your prospect will use to decide among his alternatives. If he has none, you will help him formulate them. If you know what it takes to win, by understanding his buying criteria, or helping him create them, then you can tailor your proposal to hit a home run EVERY TIME! The Vision of Solution module will show you how to accomplish this objective.

Investment

It always comes down to money. Unless a prospect can afford your offering and is willing to invest, you cannot help her. Money is always an issue and reaching agreement about investment before proposing is an important qualification step which if ignored can cost you the business. If money is going to be a problem, resolve it before your presentation or proposal. The problem will not go away simply by ignoring it. In fact, ignoring it will actually make it worse.

Decision Process

Organizations and individuals have certain ways of making decisions. Once you discover your prospect's organizational decision-making process, you can align your selling activities to perfectly mesh with their steps.

Major Contract

It's time to pause in your selling process and answer a few questions. The Major Contract step is a personal debrief, a gut check. In essence, when you can truthfully answer the qualification debrief questions, you have qualified your prospect and are ready to move to the Proof Presentation and/or trial phase.

Proof

It's now time to deliver the proof your prospect needed and to develop the conviction that your solution will exactly meet his needs. Your Proof Presentation is nothing more than a review, oral or written, of the agreements that you and your prospect have made. Nothing new goes into it. If it has not been discussed and agreed upon in advance, leave it out. It has a strong likelihood, if included, of either delaying the sale or completely killing it. NO SURPRISES!

Retention

Your solution, once implemented, will be measured. Your customer will begin determining whether or not you are meeting his criteria. When you know how you will be measured, you can begin a customer satisfaction program that will insure your long-term success.

Commitment to the Process

We cannot control outcomes. They are, unfortunately, beyond our control. What is within our control is the ability to execute our process. Remember, you cannot control people; you can only control your process. When you do that you are in control. It is almost a certainty that if you focus on the outcome, you will not execute the sales process and in most cases will lose control of the sales cycle.

Power Principle:
Commit to the process, not to the outcome.

Instead of leaving things to chance (Murphy's Law tells us we should know better), and hoping for the best, you will actually be able to accurately predict your outcomes by managing your sales interactions with this proven sales process.

Personally commit to the Discovery Selling® process of qualification. Make a personal commitment to withhold your presentation or trial until your prospect is qualified. This is not only in your best interest, but your prospect's as well.

Power Principles:
No presentations or trials for prospects who are not qualified.

Remember this important concept: *No one can force you to do something that is not in your best interest unless you let them.* The process will protect you.

MASLOW'S HIERARCHY

Discovery Selling® uses a pyramid as its visual image. This image is based upon Abraham Maslow's hierarchy of needs theory. He believed that humans have certain basic needs that are never changing and genetic in nature. The needs are both physiological and psychological and occur in all cultures. Progression through the hierarchy occurs only when the previous needs are satisfied. The hierarchy of needs can be divided into **Basic Needs** and **Growth Needs**. At the base of the hierarchy are the more powerful motivators. Those basic needs must be satisfied before higher needs emerge.

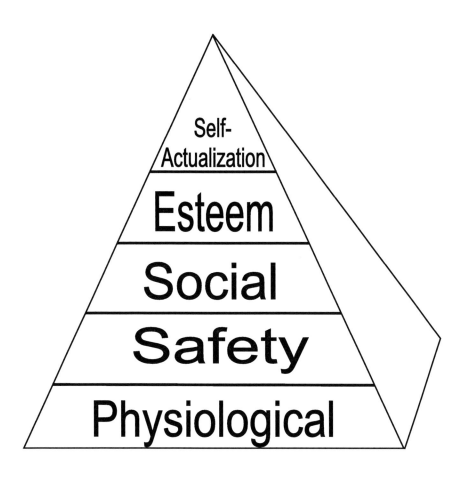

Maslow believed that man is motivated by certain needs, starting with the most basic.

Physiological Needs: include such things as food, water, air, etc. Until those needs are satisfied, nothing else seems to matter. Once the physiological needs are met, then man progresses up the hierarchy

Safety Needs: consist of feelings of safety, security, stability, and environment consistency. These needs are mostly psychological in nature. Fear can be an underlying emotion at this stage if these needs are not met.

Social Needs: love and belongingness-- In this stage, man is looking for interaction with other humans and is motivated to find fulfillment in social relationships. There is a desire to belong to group interaction.

Esteem Needs: esteem of self and esteem of others— Esteem of others is recognized through attention and recognition of others.

Self-Actualization: maximizing potential--The desire to become everything one is capable of becoming is the most complex motivator.

Progress through the levels is often interrupted. If at anytime, one's particular situation changes, one will immediately self-adjust to the level of the hierarchy that most addresses his particular situation. This fluctuation can be caused by any significant event such as divorce, loss of job, illness, etc. A great example of this was September 11th. Once the planes flew into the World Trade Center, all of our energy/motivation was focused on being safe. The victims and the survivors of September 11th were motivated by physiological needs.

The principles that apply to Maslow's Hierarchy also apply to the Discovery Selling® model. All stages of the system are progressive. Each phase must be addressed and completed prior to moving upward. Each phase has certain criteria that must be accomplished. Notice that relationship is the foundation. The Discovery Selling® Model is designed for Consultive Selling and Relationship Selling based upon business-to-business transactions.

As you progress through the manual, you will see the mini-pyramids repeated, each representing a new concept. You will see it in the Phases of Buying, in Ground Rules, in P.A.I.N., etc. Each time you see it pay particular attention to what is at the base. That is the starting point of the particular concept we are addressing. A note of caution: oftentimes, depending on timing, you may call on a prospect whom has already started the ascent.

RELATIONSHIP

What do you see when you look at this picture?

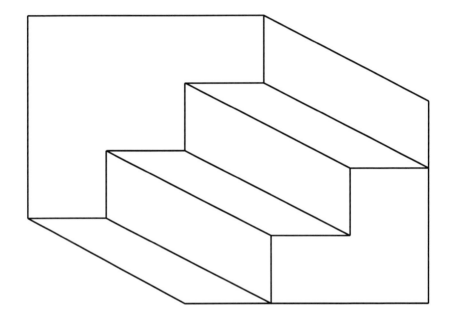

Is it a set of stairs facing up or is it a set of stairs facing down? Which is the right answer? Either is right. It is what your perception of the picture is that is the right answer

Exercise:

Write down the first five adjectives that come to your mind when you see the word EDUCATION. Now ask three other people to write down five adjectives for the word EDUCATION. What did you discover?

_____

_____

What you probably discovered from the above exercise on education was that each person you asked gave you adjectives that more often didn't match yours. Although we may hear or see the same thing someone else sees or hears, our perception of what we see or hear may be totally different from another's perception. Perception is a subjective, not an objective view of the world. This is often demonstrated when several people witness an accident. They all have somewhat different renditions of what occurred.

What does all this information have to do with sales? Sales is all about communication. Each of us has ways that we prefer to receive information and interact with people. Our job as a salesperson is to discover those preferences.

Platinum Rule

Most of us are familiar with the Golden Rule, "Do unto others as you would have them do unto you". Dr. Anthony Allessandro refers to the Platinum Rule—"Do unto other as they want to be done unto." The Platinum Rule will help you build a relationship more easily than the Golden Rule.

Our job as salespeople is to discover our prospect's

preferences in the area of communication and interaction,

and then to step into our prospect's frame of reference.

Power Principles:
All things being equal, people do business with people they trust.
All things not being equal, people do business with people they trust.
People tend to trust people who are like themselves.

The Trust Triangle

Building a relationship is a nebulous concept. So many

times, the phrase "building a relationship" is synonymous

with being friends and or being friendly with the prospect.

Being friendly with a person is nothing more than having

good interpersonal skills. We are friendly with the grocery

clerk, the waitress, and the child who comes to our door to

sell candy; however, we don't have a relationship with any of those people.

Relationship defines trust and the ability to communicate effectively. By creating the proper environment, we can have honest and open discussions about "real" issues. Relationship is not a substitute for sales skills, and should never be an end in itself. However, we won't be able to use sales skills unless we have a relationship.

Everything we do in the selling process is either strengthening the relationship or undermining it. TRUST is at the heart of all strong relationships. Trust is composed of three equally important components:

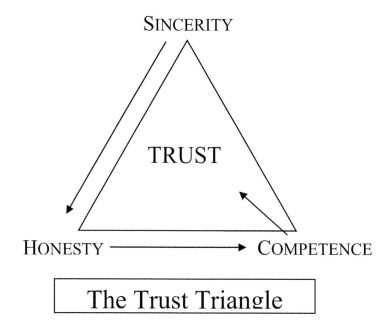

The Trust Triangle

Sincerity, Honesty, and Competence are necessary components in establishing trust. If any of the three elements are missing, a relationship cannot be formed or sustained.

A word about sincerity. Sincerity is the emotional impact one has on a person. A recent example from one of the authors serves to illustrate this point.

> *"Several years ago, I was at Grand Cayman, BWI. Everyday I would walk to the beach and pass a store that had this beautiful black coral bracelet sitting in the window beckoning to me. As I returned from the beach, I would naturally pass the jewelry store and peer once again at the bracelet. I did this for ten days. Finally, on the day we were supposed to return home, I mentioned to my husband that I would really like to have that bracelet. He suggested we leave early and on the way to the airport, stop at the store and purchase the bracelet. An interesting thing happened. We went into the jewelry store and I asked the clerk to show me the bracelet. He put it on my arm, I looked at it and then proceeded to tell him I would think it over. When we got outside, my husband looked at me and said, "What just happened? I'm confused." I told him that there was something about the man that I didn't trust. When asked to elaborate, I couldn't really be specific, but the feeling I got was that I couldn't trust him."*

The emotional impact he had on me was negative and it was over before it even got started. Judging whether we trust someone or whether we don't trust someone is a totally subjective activity. (Refer back to the three power principles on relationship).

Brunswick Lens Model

Professor Egon Brunswick, University of California at Berkeley, conceived the Lens Model and its essence is, "What we think we see in others will determine, for the most part, how we will treat them and respond to them. The accuracy of what we think we see will dictate the appropriateness of the behavior we utilize or the actions we take and the resulting productivity of the relationship."*

In a relationship, one must bond and be in rapport. What does it mean to bond and establish rapport?

To bond means *to join together*.

Rapport is a French word that's literal meaning is *to offer back*.

*Dr. Jay Hall, PhD., Models for Management: The Structure of Competence, Woodstead Press, Woodlands, Texas, (1980?-1994)

Therefore, to create a relationship we must join together and offer back. The old saying that the first five minutes of an encounter are the most important carries definite weight. When we meet someone, we either value them or place judgment upon them. We value them if they are somewhat like us and we "click". The doors of communication remain open and information can flow. On the other hand, if we meet someone who is so different than us, we become judgmental and the doors of communication are slammed shut.

The Personal Presence Pie

When we communicate with another person, we use three methods. We use our words, our tonality, and our body language. Seven percent of our ability to communicate is communicated through the words we use; thirty-eight percent of our ability to communicate is communicated through our tonality, fifty-five percent of our ability to communicate is communicated through our body language. We call this our *personal presence.*

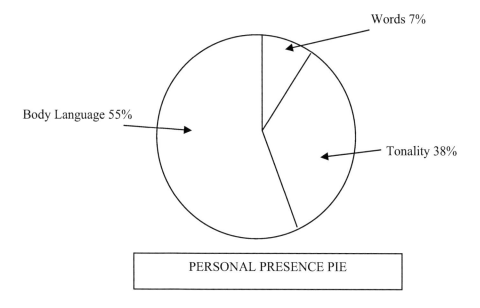

PERSONAL PRESENCE PIE

We must be aware that 93% of the communication process is conveyed through something other than words. A person's body language and tone can tell much more at times than the words he/she is using.

Since trust is what makes the sale possible, it must be established almost immediately. How do we do this? Look at Power Principle #3:

People trust people who are like themselves.

Therefore, to keep the doors of communication open, we have to act and talk more like our prospects, because, Power Principle #1:

People do business with people they trust.

Matching and mirroring can accomplish this. There are several ways to match and mirror our prospect. We can match and mirror body language, tone, pace and voice volume of the prospect. Oftentimes, we do this subconsciously. However, if we consciously match and mirror, we must do this in a manner that does not seem contrived or condescending.

The Eyes Tell The Story

A person's eye movement can give us a lot of information about that person. In sales, we can use this to read our prospect's primary processing modality; in other words, how a person processes incoming information. There are three processing modes:

Visual – Processes information by what they see

Auditory – Processes information by what they hear

Kinesthetic – Processes information by what they feel

People use their eyes to access different parts of their brain. The movement of their eyes upon asking simple questions can give you a clue as to what processing style they are using. If a person looks up and to either the right or left, they process information visually. If a person looks to either side, in the direction of their ears, they are processing in an auditory manner. If a person looks down and to the right they are processing kinesthetically. If a person looks down and to the left they are processing in auditory dialogue, also known as internalization. A person who is in auditory dialogue thinks out loud. (Refer to picture).

SIGHT
create

SIGHT
recall

SOUND
create

SOUND
recall

FEELING

INTERNALIZATION
(Sound)

Their **RIGHT** side   Their **LEFT** side

This will be reversed in a left-handed individual.

Whether a person looks to the right or left also gives vital information. Looking to the left, either up down or center, means he/she is remembering the answer. He/she has been asked this question before or has an established opinion or answer. When a person looks to the right he/she is constructing the answer. This does not necessarily mean they are lying, it could mean they have never been asked that particular question before or in that manner.

Exercise:

Ask a friend to give you his or her opinion on gun control. Be careful how you phrase your question. Don't say "How do you feel" or "Tell me about your position on gun control". If you word the question improperly, you may be predisposing the person to process a particular way. The phrase is "**Give me your opinion on gun control**." Watch the direction of his or her eyes.

Describe what you noticed and what processing mode the person used.

_____

_____

_____

_____

_____

Another way to identify processing styles is in verbal cues the prospect gives. They will use certain words that will give you cues to their style. A person who processes visually will use visual oriented words such as _look, see, envision, view, visualize and color._ An auditory person will use sound oriented words such as _tell, loud, talk, hear, listen, say, speak and explain._ A kinesthetic person will use feeling words such *as feel, touch, handle, push, pressure, uncomfortable, grasp and guts.*

Additional Identification Tips

In addition to eye movement and verbal cues, notice the pacing or speed at which the person speaks. Visuals talk quite rapidly since they are describing visual images in their brain. As such, they progress quickly in their speaking pace. Auditories choose their words carefully and like to use words appropriately. As a consequence, they speak at a slightly slower pace than visuals. Kinesthetics typically have the slowest pace and also tend to be the most soft-spoken of the three types.

Application

By using the previous information, you are equipped to begin the relationship-building process from the very first interaction with a prospect.

If the person is visual, the salesperson should use visual words and phrases. "Nice to see you," or "How does this look?" or "Do you get the picture?" .

If the person is auditory, the salesperson should use sound oriented words and phrases. "Nice hearing from you," or "How does that sound?" or "Is this resonating?" or "Does this ring a bell?"

If the person is kinesthetic, the salesperson should use feeling or touch-based words and phrases. "How do you feel about that?" or "Let's stay in touch," or "Will you be able to get your arms around this?"

In addition to modifying your words and phrases slightly, your speaking pace should approximate the speed of the other person. Typically, visuals speak quickly and often use incorrect words; auditories speak at a slower and a precise rate; and kinesthetics will speak the slowest and softest. Matching the voice characteristics of the other person can pay big relationship dividends later.

Other Tips to Building a Relationship

Visuals judge everything on looks or appearances and often they must see things to understand them. It is often not uncommon for a *visual* to say, "I can't see what you're saying." What that person is telling you is that they need to see it. Therefore, pictures, charts, written information, will all be important to a visual person's understanding of what you are selling. In addition, your personal appearance is extremely important to a visual. It is important to understand however, that a *visual* will judge you on your appearance. Once relationship is firmly established, you might be able to relax a bit. Finally*, visuals* want eye contact. Whereas *auditories* and *kinesthetics* may find that unimportant and even distracting. *Visuals* measure another person on the level of their eye contact. Look at them when you're talking to them or when they are talking to you. The majority of the adult population (55%) is visual, so you will probably be working in this modality most of the time.

Auditories have less need to see things. Therefore, even if you show them something, explain it as well. They need to hear it. When presenting or conversing with an *auditory*, try to do so in a quiet environment. Noisy backgrounds in crowded places such as restaurants, bars, sporting events or other such places are extremely distracting to an *auditory*. Since they are extremely sensitive to sounds and have difficulty filtering out background noise, try to pick a place and a time for interaction that will provide a supportive dialogue. Another characteristic of *auditories* that might seem bothersome is their lack of eye contact. Instead, they tilt their heads and often turn one of their ears toward you when listening. Do not make the mistake of thinking they are not paying attention because they are. If your personal style is auditory, you may need to practice making more consistent eye contact with others, particularly visuals. And one final note, choose your words well. *Auditories* will often become distracted by the misuse or mispronunciations of words. In fact, they will often correct the other person. If you are an *auditory*, be careful of this tendency. Your correction may be right, but you may lose in the process because of the negative feelings this might create in the other person.

Kinesthetics are slow decision makers that are always measuring how they are feeling about something. Emotions are often mixed and thus confusing and it takes *kinesthetics* more time than either of the other styles to make assessments. The *kinesthetic* will use both visual and auditory modes to receive information, but must then take time to process it to determine feelings. The most important thing to remember is not to pressure them. They will become highly resistant in the face of pressure and it could cost you a sale that might otherwise be made. *Kinesthetics* are touch-oriented, so don't be surprised if they move in close to you to create an atmosphere of intimacy. While *visuals* want you outside of "their space", *kinesthetics* want you "inside their space" and will usually move toward you during a conversation. During the meeting, they usually will move over to the other side of the desk to remove physical barriers.

Through the disciplined application of this information, you will begin to "read" people at a level far deeper than most others, and you will connect or bond with that person in an almost magical way. In terms of building relationships, it is important to remember people are suspicious of people they don't know. By breaking through that barrier and eliminating the prospect's perception that "you are different than me", you will begin building a trust relationship that will ultimately make the buyer/seller interaction highly productive and mutually profitable.

Ground Rules
Relationship

GROUND RULES

When a boxing match is about to begin, the referee calls both boxers to the center of the ring. What is the referee doing?   He is establishing the rules of the fight. Laying down the ground rules also occurs in various other sports such as football and baseball. Undoubtedly, the sportsmen know the rules; however, they are continually repeated to avoid any misunderstandings. Why? All parties need to know and agree to the expectations set in the pre-game discussion.

When children get together to play a game, you often hear them discuss the rules together. If you ever get the opportunity to listen to the interaction you will hear all parties describe in detail what they are actually expecting to happen during their game.

When you go to a dentist, the dentist will look in your mouth and if you need a filling, he will tell you exactly what the process is going to be. He will tell you that he is going to put a topical anesthetic on your gum, then give you a shot of Novocain. When your gum is nice and numb he will then start the drilling and repair your cavity. He will also assure you that if at any time you feel pain he'll stop and give you more Novocain. The dentist does this to alleviate fears and to create a level of comfort, so you know what is happening at all times.

Setting the Ground Rules is a technique used to create comfort and to eliminate misunderstandings. Ground Rules also allow all parties involved to know what is happening and what is expected. In addition, either party has the right at any time to end the interaction without the feeling of being held captive. Setting Ground Rules creates a solid, open line of communication.

Setting the Ground Rules also helps build the relationship. (If you recall, a relationship is based upon trust: Sincerity, Honesty, and Competence. Sincerity is the emotional impact you have on another person). Ground Rules need to be established on every sales call. All parties need to agree upon what is going to occur and what is going to be accomplished in the allotted time spent together. In so doing, you are honoring the prospect and letting him know that you recognize his time is important. You are also showing him through your actions, that you want to address his concerns--even though his concerns may differ from yours. This is also an opportunity to give him a "stroke", a form of recognition.

Unfortunately, however, too often the salesperson begins the interaction with the prospect by going into the salesperson "Spew". Talking more than the prospect, being insensitive to the prospects time restrictions, and not determining exactly what the prospect would like to accomplish during the time he is together with the salesperson. In essence, the salesperson is on his agenda and is not sensitive to the prospects needs. The salesperson breaks the 75/25-power principle. *

*Power Principle:
The salesperson should listen 75% of the time, and talk 25% of the time. Conversely, the prospect should be talking 75% of the time and listening 25% of the time.

Establishing the BBI

All buyer-seller interactions must have a central purpose, a stated objective for the meeting. That purpose is called the Basic Business Issue (BBI). The BBI is the primary reason that a buyer might want to meet with you or any salesperson. The BBI is the central focus of the conversation and not only sets the tone of the conversation, but also clearly defines the meeting agenda as well as the potential outcome, which is agreeable to both parties. Without establishing the BBI, it is difficult to develop a focus for the conversation. The BBI establishes the Premise of the Call.

There is a reason the prospect is meeting with you. It may be just to find out a little about your company because he may have a potential need. It might be because he has a major problem and needs help. It could be that his superior has asked him to get information. It could be any number of reasons. One thing is for certain; he is not seeing you just because he is a nice guy and needs to waste 45 minutes of his day. *

*Power Principle:
All human behavior is purposeful.
All human behavior has a positive intent.

Your job as a competent salesperson is to determine what the prospect's BBI is. In addition, as a competent salesperson, you should know what your objective is before you begin the call. Too many times, salespeople go into a call, begin to talk (spew), leave, and feel that they have had a productive meeting. In reality, they didn't connect with the prospect and address the prospect's needs (BBI).

Framing the Call

The Ground Rules, just like in a boxing match, need to be established in the initial meeting with a prospect. The following format is designed to let both parties know what will happen during and after the initial meeting. Ground Rules can be established through a five-step process. The acronym T.T.A.P.E. will help you remember the steps.

Thank You: An initial bonding and rapport step to lower resistance and help the prospect become comfortable enough to share information.

"Thanks for inviting me in today." Or, *"Thank you for taking the time to visit with me."*

Notice the word *inviting* and *visit*. There is a reason to use these specific words. People treat invited guests differently than they do salespeople. Let's pretend your former boss, whom you respect greatly, happens to be passing through your town and calls you. He is going to be in town just for the day and you invite him over to your house for a drink. Your first impulse, if you were a woman, would be to go home and make sure your house is in order and looks presentable for company. (If you are a man, it may not ever cross your mind). After you are sure your house is presentable, you remember that your boss enjoys a good glass of red wine. Chances are, you will make sure you have a decent red wine on hand and probably some munchies to go along with it.
Your boss arrives at the agreed upon time and you offer him a glass of wine, which he readily accepts, and you invite him into your living room to sit down and chat. You are particularly proud of your living room because you have just invested in some new white

carpet. As you are visiting, your boss has an accident and spills the red wine on your new white carpet. What do you say to him? Do you say, "Oh you klutz, that is my new carpeting," or do you say, "That's OK, I'll just get a towel and wipe it up. No problem." Chances are you will say some version of the latter response. Why? Because we treat invited guests differently than we treat uninvited guests. Invited guests are welcomed, uninvited guests are an intrusion.

After thanking the prospect for inviting you in, make sure you pause 4-5 seconds to wait for a response. Oftentimes, the prospect will send you a signal of how he would like to proceed. His response will tell you if he is Time/Task oriented and wants to get down to business or if he is People/Relationship oriented and would like to "chit-chat" before proceeding. His response will give you an indication of his particular behavioral style. Through observation, you will be able to determine what type of behavior style you need to adapt in order to implement the "Platinum Rule." As the salesperson, your job is to keep the doors of communication open to allow information to flow.

Time Frame: To reach an understanding of the projected length of time for the meeting.

"How much time do you see us spending together today?"

There is nothing more aggravating to a person with a busy schedule than to have her time monopolized by a salesperson. If the prospect says that she put aside twenty minutes for your time together, then you as a salesperson need make sure you stick to the allotted time. After twenty minutes, you need to stop and tell the prospect you have reached the allotted time. If you are having a worthwhile conversation, from the prospect's perspective, she will tell you to continue with the meeting. If on the other hand, she has another appointment or simply wants to end the meeting for whatever reason, then you are being sensitive to her needs. What you do always speaks louder than what you say. How honest is it to ask the prospect how much time she put aside for the meeting, to tell her you will adhere to her time constraints, and then when your time is up to ignore your commitment? *

*Power Principle:
Behavior is the true measure of intent.

Accomplish: To reach an understanding about what the prospect wants to accomplish in the meeting.

"What is it you were hoping to accomplish in our time together today?"

We know all human behavior is purposeful, so it is important to find out what in particular the prospect is hoping to accomplish by meeting with you. Sometimes the prospect will tell you that she just wants to know a little more about your company. Sometimes the prospect will say that you made the call and she thought she would see what you have. Sometimes she will start telling you about some of her "P.A.I.N." and ask if you can help.

The major reason to ask her about her objective is to give you some indication of where to start when you actually begin visiting about her particular situation. What she mentions is the issue that is most important to her.

One of the author's relates the following example:

> *"I was on one appointment that was set for me by my assistant. The President of a welding company called the office and said he wanted someone to come out and see him. My assistant readily set up*

the time for us to meet. When I walked into his office, I thanked him for taking the time to visit with me. At that point, he said that he had been saving the faxes that my office had been sending to him as a form of marketing. He pointed to the statements about sales improvement and asked where we came off making them. He was quite impatient.

At this juncture, most salespeople would start "spewing" and begin defending those statements. The first thing I did was thank him for saving my faxes, and then I asked him to explain which of the statement were most upsetting. He told me. Then I asked him why those particular statements caught his eye. He then started telling me what was happening in his company. He had a high level of P.A.I.N. and was extremely aggravated with his situation.

The reason I share this story with you is to illustrate that in this particular instance, it would not have been appropriate to ask him what he wanted to accomplish. He had already told me in an indirect way.

This particular person was very assertive. Had I started defending my statements, I probably would have been out of his office in fifteen minutes. Consequently, by being tuned in to this person's needs and addressing those needs in a meaningful way resulted in a two-year corporate contract.

Permission: To get permission to ask questions to understand the prospect's situation--what's working, what's important, what's not working, etc.

> *"Would you be comfortable if I asked you some questions to get a better understanding of your world? I'd also like you to ask me some questions. Would you do that?"*

Questions can be abrasive and easily turn into an interrogation. Therefore, it is important to gain permission to ask questions. Also, by encouraging the person to ask you questions, you are creating an even playing field in the prospect's mind. You are not asking him or her to do something you are not agreeing to do also.

In order to ask the right questions, however, it is imperative you listen intently to what the prospect is saying. Competence is demonstrated by asking the **right** questions the **right** way and at the **right** time. You won't be able to do that unless you listen. Too often, salespeople will hear an indicator of a problem, and rush in to give a solution without truly determining the real problem.

Example:

If you go to a doctor and tell the doctor that you have a pain in your right side and he immediately responds, "That's easy, we will make an appointment for surgery and take out your appendix. You will be as good as new." Your first thought is, "I think I need a second opinion".

On the other hand, let's assume you go to another doctor with the same problem and the doctor asks you a series of questions. "How long you have had the pain?" "Have you done any type of physical activity that may have caused the pain?"; "Have you eaten anything that may have caused the pain?"; you might think this doctor more competent than the first because he took the time to determine what your real problem was. He did that by asking questions. It may very well be that you do have to have your appendix out, but chances are you would feel safer with doctor #2. The difference between the doctor in the first scenario and the second doctor is that doctor #2 did a thorough diagnosis, while, doctor #1 rushed to a solution.

In order to determine how you can best help the prospect you need to ask questions. Set the stage in the beginning of the sales call by getting permission. It will pay off later in the call.

End: To reach agreement that by the end of the meeting the prospect and salesperson will have decided whether or not to pursue anything further or to develop a clear plan that specifically defines the next steps.

"At the end of our time together, we can decide whether or not there is a next step and what it might be."

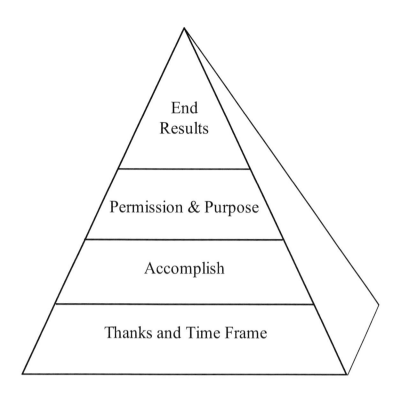

Testing Commitment

There are 4 possible positive outcomes to any sales encounter. The first outcome is a YES. All of us want every sales encounter to be a sale. Unfortunately, that is not realistic. We see more people who do not qualify rather than people who do qualify.

The second possible positive outcome is a NO. Why is a NO positive? It helps eliminate the chase. NO allows you to move on to the next prospect. Salespeople waste far too much time with prospects that will never buy. To be truly efficient as a salesperson, it is imperative that you have a qualification process that allows for a series of commitments from both parties. If a prospect were never going to buy, wouldn't you rather know that early in the sales process, rather than later?

The third possible positive outcome is a CLEAR NEXT STEP. How many times have you walked away from a sales call wondering what is going to happen next? By asking the question *"What's the next step?"* both parties will end the meeting knowing what is going to happen next and who is responsible for what. Those four important words will also show you the prospect's level of commitment.

The fourth possible positive outcome is a lesson. Learn a lesson from the sales call. What did you do right? What did you do wrong? Debrief the call and learn a lesson. It is the only way to continually improve and move closer to the mastery level.

From Soaps to Strokes

From Soaps to Strokes

Selling revolves around effective communication. In order to communicate effectively, it is necessary to have a Sender, Receiver, and Feedback. It is in the manner the sender sends information, the receiver receives information and dialogue (feedback) that occurs between the two, which will ultimately determine whether or not there is true communication.

Dr. Thomas Harris, in his book I'm OK- You're OK, contends that all relationships are strongly influenced by how you view yourself (OK or not OK) and by how you view other people. Dr. Eric Berne, in his book Games People Play, focuses on patterns of action that people display repeatedly. Together, Dr. Berne and Dr. Harris, through their extensive work in *Transactional Analysis*, have equipped us with powerful tools for effective communication, which is the essence of selling.

When given a choice, people want to feel OK about themselves, rather than Not OK about themselves. Words that describe OK'ness are: happy, comfortable, relaxed, and non-threatened. This sense of OK'ness is communicated through the words we use, the body language we exhibit, and the tone of our voice. Words that describe not-OK'ness are words such as: sad, tense, stressed etc. These feelings are also communicated through our words, body language and tonality.

One's feeling of OK'ness is on a continuum. The way most people maintain their OK'ness is to compare themselves to people who are less OK than them. This can be illustrated by the popularity of Soap Operas and some TV talk shows. Why do so many people watch Soap Operas and daytime talk shows? Because as they are watching the horrible things that happen to the fictional or real-life characters, they're thinking at a subconscious level, that even though things are not going as well as they would like for themselves, at least their life is not as bad as these other people's. Therefore, their OK'ness goes up.

Example of the OK'ness Continuum

John Doe is an outside salesman whose job is to make sales calls in his territory all day. He is required to see at least 10 people per day. When he left the office in the morning he was upbeat and expected to make at least one sale (OK'ness High). As the day went on, no one was receptive to his ideas and at about 3:00 it was apparent that today he was not going to make a sale (OK'ness Moderately Low). At around 3:30 he dragged himself back to the office to take care of some paperwork (OK'ness Low).

When he entered the office, he noticed three telephone messages in his slot. They were from people who wanted to talk to him. Being an optimist, John thought that all the hard work from his efforts was finally going to pay off (OK'ness High). John walks back to his desk and makes the first call. The person's name was Sue Smith. He dialed the phone and anticipated the best. Sue answered the phone and told John that she was with the mortgage company and that she was informing him that they were starting proceedings to foreclose on his house (OK'ness Low). John asked that she hold off because he was about to receive a large commission check that would allow him to pay his back payments and get caught up. Sue told him they would wait

seven day before starting the process (OK'ness Very Low).
John hung up the phone and felt that he had a reprieve.

He picked up his next message and debated whether to call. His thoughts were that certainly this message would bring good news. The next person was Jack Jones. Jack also answered his phone and the minute John heard the company Jack was with, he knew it was the bank that held the note on his car. They too, were probably going to give him unpleasant news. John politely indicated that he had dialed the wrong number and hung up. Just as he did, he noticed the payroll clerk coming toward him with his check. This was the day commissions were paid (OK'ness Going Up). John opened the envelope and noticed his commission was a fraction of what he thought it would be (OK'ness coming down fast). John asked why he wasn't paid what he had earned and the payroll clerk told him he had turned in his paperwork late and he would have to wait until next payday (OK'ness in the dump). At this point John decided to leave work and stop off at the nearest bar.

John went into the bar and sat down. Seated next to him was a man who asked John how his day had gone. John lamented the terrible chain of events of the day. After John was finished with his tale of woe, the man looked him in the eye and said, "At least you have a job, a car, and a house. I lost my job and my car several months ago. My wife has left me and my family thinks I am a miserable failure." Suddenly, John found someone worse off than him and started feeling better (OK'ness Moving Up).

Application

How does all this information relate to sales? Our job, as salespeople is to keep the doors of communication open. It is the two-way flow of information that will help us determine what the prospect's particular issues are and also determine whether or not we can help them.

Will a prospect share information if our behavior causes him/her to go Not-OK? The obvious answer is no. In addition, if we cause our prospect to feel Not-OK, he/she will have to find a way to achieve OK'ness. That might be at the salesperson's expense.

Exercise:

List some behaviors that salespeople do that might create uncomfortable feelings for customers and prospects.

1. _____

2. _____

3. _____

4. _____

5. _____

6. _____

List some behaviors that customers and prospects do to create uncomfortable feelings for us as salespeople.

1. _____

2. _____

3. _____

4. _____

5. _____

6. _____

Recognizing the behaviors that cause us to feel nervous, insecure, angry etc. will help us become purposeful in our responses.

Oftentimes, in our struggles to feel better, we adopt behavior that in turn will put the prospect in an uncomfortable position. In so doing, we might initially make ourselves feel better, but it will be at another's expense. Consequently, we inadvertently close the doors of communication and most likely, lose the chance of doing business.

To understand this further, it is helpful to explore the four possible psychological positions that you and your prospect will feel at any given time. The four "life positions", from Dr. Thomas Harris' I'm OK-You're OK, are repositioned in the arena of sales addressing interaction between the salesperson and the prospect or client.

Position 1: I'm OK- You're Not OK*

In this position the salesperson will do or say something that causes the prospect to become uncomfortable, or not OK, usually as a means of increasing his OK'ness.

It is particularly important for a salesperson to be cognizant of this psychological position while probing for P.A.I.N. A prospect will not share his P.A.I.N. with you if he feels threatened in any way, or if he feels you will use the information to your advantage and to his disadvantage.

Laying the ground rules in the beginning of the call will contribute to your prospect maintaining his OK position. Ground Rules give the prospect a feeling of control over his environment. If you recall, T.T.A.P.E. stands for Thanks, Time, Accomplish, Permission, and End. The first "T" is an opportunity to give the prospect a stroke. The second "T" allows the prospect to set the time limitations to the meeting. The "A" offers the opportunity to the prospect to dictate to you what he would like to accomplish in your time together. The "P" gives the prospect the opportunity to ask you questions.   Questions can be abrasive and can be interpreted as an interrogation.   Getting permission to ask questions will help the prospect feel that the questions are sincere and are in his best interest.

Position 2: I'm Not OK-You're OK*

It is crucial for the salesperson to maintain his OK position at all times.

Your job on a sales call is to be a facilitator in the discovery process to help the prospect determine if indeed there is a reason to explore the possibility of doing business with you.

The only way to accomplish that is to ask the right questions, the right way, at the right time, and to listen intently. Listening intently is the precursor to proper questioning and is often the most difficult skill to master. Too often, a prospect may say or do something to cause you to stop listening to him and to start listening to your self through your "self-talk". That self-talk may sound something like: "He doesn't like me. He'll get mad at me. Who does he think he is? Oh no, he is not going to buy!" etc. When this happens you are on your way to feeling Not-OK and definitely not listening.

Power Principle:
Check your feelings at the door

Position 3: I'm Not OK- You're Not OK*

When this psychological position occurs, there is a total breakdown in communication. Both parties may be angry, hurt, fearful, etc. When these feelings arise, the response from either party will be flight or fight.

Example:

A customer calls the salesperson because of a breakdown in service. The machine that the customer bought which was *supposed to be* top of the line and was definitely top dollar, ceased to work. When the service department was called, their response was that it would be at least 48 hours before they could service the machine. That would leave the customer in a bind and with down time. Down time would cause the customer to lose money. The customer goes Not-OK. He has to get his OK'ness back, so he calls the salesperson and unloads on him. He even goes so far as to call the salesperson dishonest. The salesperson allows himself to go Not-OK and starts defending his company, his product and the service department. That action forces the customer to hang up on the salesperson and call the salesperson's boss.

The saga will continue until the situation is handled in a manner that will help the prospect to regain his OK'ness.

Power Principle:
Customers go away because they don't feel appreciated or understood

Power Principle:
Your best customers are your competitor's best prospects.

Position 4: I'm OK, You're OK*

True communication occurs in this psychological state. All the relationships you have with a prospect/client are strongly influenced by a combination of how you, as a salesperson, view yourself and how you view your prospect/client. Conversely, your prospect/client is also affected by the same criteria. Therefore, as salespeople we always want to act in a manner that will keep the prospect/client in an OK position.

You have probably been able to determine that the Discovery Selling® system is designed to help the prospect stay in an OK position. Building a trust relationship, laying the ground rules, helping the prospect to create his vision of solution, are designed to create a win/win outcome.

*For more information on psychological states refer to I'm OK, You're OK, by Dr. Thomas Harris.

The Sales Rescue

Unfortunately, there are times that situations or events occur that cause the prospect to go Not OK. If you remember the principle of OK'ness, the way people get their OK'ness is to find people who are less OK than them. So, when your prospect becomes not OK, your job is to *appear* less OK than them. Notice the word is *appear*. We always have to maintain our OK'ness inside; however, we just **act** a little less OK than the prospect. In so doing, you go into the "Sales Rescue" role. The Sales Rescue theory rests on the fact that when someone needs help, most of us as human beings will offer it. Examples appear daily in the news, where total strangers have risked their own safety to save or help others. It seems most of us have this instinct programmed into our DNA.

The following six statements, if delivered properly, will precipitate the Sales Rescue:

1. I'm confused

2. It's my fault.

3. I take full responsibility.

4. I have a problem.

5. I need your help.

6. I'm surprised.

Example:

Some of the older detective shows on TV often illustrate this principle. Columbo and Matlock are perfect examples of acting a little less OK. Columbo was forgetful and always struggled. In so doing, he would always be able to extricate more information-- information that would ultimately lead to capturing the murderer. Matlock was the country bumpkin who acted like he was clueless about what was occurring around him. In so doing, people lowered their defenses and gave him information that would lead to their conviction. Neither Columbo nor Matlock appeared to pose a threat to their suspects. They just asked lots of questions, in an attempt to understand. They did not appear to have all the answers.

Please understand that we are not advocating that you begin acting like Columbo or Matlock. What we are advocating is that you use their principles. Columbo and Matlock are used merely as examples, solely to make a point.

Nevertheless, there are times that it is appropriate for a salesperson to intentionally act a little less OK than the prospect, to help the prospect feel OK. The intent of acting a little less-Ok is to keep the doors of communication open thus maintaining a flow of information.

Sample Rescue Phrases:

"Danielle, I'm a bit confused. My understanding was that I was going to hear from you today. My fault, I must have written the wrong date."

"John, I forget, did we discuss how much time we wanted to spend together today?"

"Lisa, I apologize. You're upset with me."

"Bill, I have a problem and I need your help. It's my fault and I take full responsibility for it. I said something that upset you and I don't know what it was. Could you help me out?"

"Betty, you say that you're still considering my proposal. I'm surprised to hear you say that."

As you read these statements, some of you are probably

thinking that you would never use these phrases. Others of

you are probably thinking that you use these statements or a

variation of them all of the time.

Why will it be difficult for some of you and not others?

How you react to the statements depends upon your

behavioral style. All of us have a core style in which we most comfortably act. Similar styles exhibit similar behavior traits. We get our behavioral style from a combination of our training, our environment, and our heredity.

Behavioral Style

Hippocrates first observed behavioral styles in 400 B.C. He contended that he could predict which armies in battle would win simply by watching their observable behavior within their environment. From these observations, he was able to identify four types of temperaments: Sanguine, Melancholic, Choleric, and Phlegmatic.

This form of typing is sometimes referred to as personality styles. Personality is far more complex and in most instances not possible to type. Behavior, on the other hand, is *situational and observable.* It is imperative that we take these two factors into consideration when we seek to identify a person's preferred mode of behavior.

Fast-forward in history and Carl Jung appeared around 1921. Jung also identified four types of behavior but attributed each behavior to the psychological attributes of feeling, thinking, sensation and intuition. He indicated two of the four styles would be extroverted, while the remaining two styles would be introverted. In extroversion, energy is directed outward to the environment, in introversion energy is directed inward toward self and thinking.

In 1928, William Moulton Marston developed the DISC language, and published his findings in <u>The Emotions of Normal People</u>. DISC is defined as a universal language of observable behavior. DISC does not measure intelligence, skills, education, or values. It simply will indicate how a person will act in a given situation. It is important to remember, as quoted from W.M. Marston, "All people exhibit all four behavioral factors in varying degrees of intensity." Typically, one particular factor or dimension of behavior is more predominant in all of our behavior, and that is the individual's "core" style.

For our purposes, we will use the DISC model. The DISC model is user friendly and will help you become aware of yourself, but more importantly become aware of your prospect. Becoming aware of your prospect's preferred behavioral style can only help in keeping the doors of communication open and thus aide in building the trust relationship.

The four basic styles are Dominant, Influencer, Steady Relater, and Conscientious. Each style is characterized by distinct behavioral characteristics. Each style has a basic motivator, an underlying dominant emotion, and common characteristics. Each of the four styles has an "I am" statement that serves to describe that particular style's self-perception.

Dominant

"I am powerful."

The Dominant style is motivated by solving problems. They like the challenge, they are big picture, and they will take risks. They are results oriented and time/task oriented. Their underlying emotion is anger. They are impatient people who have a short fuse. Note, they don't go around angry all the time, but are quick to anger when in a stressful situation. Many times the Dominant style has learned to mask that anger. Nevertheless, the emotion will still occur. Some descriptors are assertive, goal oriented, and direct. They view their environment as antagonistic. Their conflict response is to fight. Their pace is quick and deliberate. They show irritation or impatience when people waste their time, beat around the bush and don't mirror their sense of urgency. They want to see results.

Dominants represent 18% of population.

Influencer

"I am happy."

The Influencer is motivated and energized by being around people. They are outgoing, animated and can be very persuasive. They have a strong need for verbal interaction, thus they work best when interacting with other people rather than alone. This style is often referred to as the "expressive" style. You can usually spot an Influencer by their animated facial expressions and their upbeat demonstrative behavior. Their underlying emotion is optimism and they tend to be very trusting of others. Their needs-driven behavior is to talk (verbalize) and they too are big picture (less detail oriented). They are motivated by praise and positive strokes (social recognition) and are people/relationship oriented. Some descriptors are charismatic, warm and enthusiastic. They view their environment as favorable. Their conflict response is flight or to flee from an unpleasant situation. Their pace is quick and lighthearted. They enjoy interaction that is emotionally stimulating. There's always time for a good laugh.

Influencers represent 28% of the population.

Steady Relater

"I am dependable."

The Steady Relater is motivated by closure and maintaining an even steady pace. They like to establish repetitive patterns to accomplish tasks and will follow those patterns predictably with great patience. They like routine. Their needs driven behavior is to serve and help other people. They are exceptional team players and are excellent listeners. Their underlying emotion is "non-emotion," or passiveness. It is not that a Steady Relater doesn't feel emotions; they have feelings of anger, happiness, sadness, etc. just like anyone else. However, Steady Relaters are excellent at masking their emotions. They view their environment as favorable, and are people/relationship oriented. They do not like confrontation and hostility and will avoid engaging in behaviors which are confrontational.

Some descriptors of Steady Relaters are methodical, patient, and deliberate. They view their environment as friendly, however are introverted. Their conflict response is to tolerate or acquiesce. In acquiescence, they become overly passive. Their pace is slow and even-tempered and they show concern for others. It is important to remember that it is hard for a Steady Relater to say no.

Steady Relaters represent 40% of population.

Conscientious

"I am accurate."

The Conscientious Thinker is motivated by following procedures. They often strive to find better ways of doing things. They are detail oriented and need facts, lots of them, to make a decision. They are task/time oriented and view their environment as antagonistic. Their underlying emotion is fear. They fear making a mistake. They have a difficult time delegating tasks because they tend to worry that the task won't be completed properly. They are not risk-takers and don't particularly like change. Their conflict response is avoidance. For that reason, it is very difficult to push a Conscientious into making a decision, particularly if they have not had enough "thinking time" or enough facts to ponder and analyze. Some descriptors are analytical, systematic, accurate and introverted. Their pace is slow and thoughtful. They pride themselves on their analytical abilities. They methodically and laboriously explain concepts in great detail. They tend to be extremely logical and are very uncomfortable with emotional appeals. They do not trust emotions and are therefore guided by logic.

The Conscientious style represents 14% of the population.

Application

How can we use this information to help us in sales? Let's review the power principles from the Relationship section.

- All things being equal, people do business with people they trust.

- All things not being equal, people still do business with people they trust.

- People tend to trust people who are most like themselves.

It also seems an appropriate time to revisit the Tony Allesandro's Platinum Rule.

- Do unto others, as they want to be done unto.

Taking these four principles into account should help lead you to an understanding of how important it is to match and mirror other people. How would you, as a salesperson, be able to determine what a person's core style is in an expedient amount of time? There is a relatively easy way to assess the person to whom you are selling.

The DISC model is based upon two dimensions of behavior, *responsiveness* and *assertiveness*.

The first dimension, plotted on a vertical line, is the dimension of *Responsiveness*. The responsiveness scale reflects a person's openness or "warmth" to others. Does the person stay somewhat distant, focused strictly on business (Time/Task), or does she display a level of openness to connecting with the person and building a relationship People/Relationship)? Most individuals will display one of these behaviors when you meet with them. Time/Task people are formal and stick to business. They dislike small-talk and feel it's a waste of time. People/Relationship people like the social aspects of a meeting and will be far less rigid and formal in the meeting.

The second dimension of behavior is *Assertiveness*. Does the person assert, that is talk a lot, state opinions and generally takes charge; or is the person more quiet and unassuming? Assertive people will try to dominate meetings through their outspokenness and statement of opinions. Less assertive or passive individuals will be soft-spoken, with a much slower and soft-spoken pace.

By noting these behaviors, plotted as shown in the following graph, it is easy to "read" a person's core style, and adapt to that style for more effective communication.

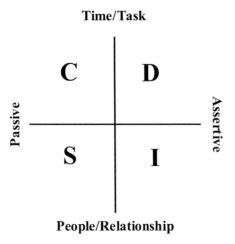

Time/Task

C | D

Passive | Assertive

S | I

People/Relationship

If a person takes control of the meeting and wants to get down to business, along with being extroverted and forceful, chances are he is a Dominant.

If a person is relatively friendly, shows a lot of expression, and is extroverted and wants to start the meeting "chit-chatting", he/she is probably an Influencer.

If a person is friendly but reserved and allows you to take the lead, chances are that person is a Steady-Relater.

Finally, if a person is task/time oriented, fairly introverted, and not quite as talkative and doesn't spend much time on small talk, he/she is probably a Conscientious.

How do you move into their world? You do that by first assessing what style they are. Laying the Ground Rules in the beginning of the call will help you in this endeavor. Watching the prospects reaction and response will help you make a quick determination as to how you should behave.

Dominants like Ground Rules because it gives them a sense of control. They often will tell you what they want to accomplish in the meeting.

Influencers like Ground Rules because it helps them stay focused to the task at hand. Ground rules will help both the prospect and you accomplish the BBI.

Steady Relaters like the Ground Rules because it allows them to know exactly what is going to occur in the meeting and lowers their fear of being pushed into doing something.

Conscientious types like the Ground Rules because it gives them the structure they want and allows for them to get down to business.

Success in selling comes from your ability to adapt your style to your prospects style.

When selling to a Dominant

- Be direct (don't beat around the bush)
- Give options
- Don't waste time
- Don't be indecisive
- Give them the information they need but don't over inform. It will bore them

When selling to an Influencer

- Spend time socializing

- Have fun on the call

- Realize that they most often make buying decisions based on feelings

- Show them innovative products if possible

- Don't give too many details.   They will get bored.

When selling to a Steady Relater

- Move a little slower

- Don't try to close too early

- Give assurances

- Give a full explanation

- Give them time to think it over

When selling to a Conscientious

- Get down to business

- Give detail

- Don't talk feelings

- Be methodical

- Be accurate in your statements

Revisiting the <u>Sales Rescue</u>

Let's look at the six statements that are suggested for the
Sales Rescue:

1. I'm confused

2. It's my fault.

3. I take full responsibility

4. I have a problem.

5. I need your help.

6. I'm surprised.

Given what you know now about psychological positions and behavior style, which styles will have the most problem using these statements? The Dominant and the Conscientious will have the most difficult time. The Dominant is assertive by nature and the Conscientious fears making a mistake.

After reading about behavioral style, you were probably able to recognize your own style. If you believe you are a Dominant or a Conscientious, understand you will have the most discomfort in using these statements. One bit of advice: you must learn to GET OVER IT! **Effective selling is about the Prospect's comfort, not the salesperson's comfort**.

Power Principle:
Human behavior is predictable.

The Sales Rescue will help you achieve the results you are looking for when you have a breakdown in communication. The big question is, are you selling for your good feelings (strokes), or are you selling to make money?

I'M OK, YOU'RE OK SALES PRINCIPLES

1. Never defend your position. By defending your position you are forcing the prospect to defend his position. It is a no-win situation. When someone comes at you, simply listen to what he is saying and move on from there.

2. Struggle intelligently, on purpose. A good time to use this principle is when there are inconsistencies in what your prospect is telling you. You know what the prospect said isn't congruent with what you have

observed and have discovered in your meeting. The words, "I don't understand," will keep him talking.

3. Memorize these words. "I don't know." Oftentimes, in the very beginning of a call, the prospect may say something along the line of, "How can you help me?" The temptation is so great to go into the spew. It would be more appropriate to say, "I don't know. Could we spend our time together today exploring that

4. When under pressure or facing an angry or hostile customer or prospect, fall back.

5. Accept strokes graciously, but always give them back. Remember, if a prospect gives you a stroke, that is your payment. So, when a prospect says

something like, "You have been so helpful." You should respond by thanking her for communicating her needs to you so openly.

6. No buzzwords. Salespeople like to use buzzwords because it makes them feel smart (OK). Unfortunately, if your prospect doesn't know what your buzzwords mean, they stop listening to you and start trying to figure out the exact meaning of the buzzword.

7. Never put a prospect or customer in a position she/he doesn't want to be in.

8. Nurture, nurture, nurture. Everyone is stroke deprived. It's particularly important to nurture in the P.A.I.N. step. When your customer/prospect

indicates to you through body language, words, or tonality they are becoming Not-OK, it is at this point you consciously nurture them. Some sample phrases might be "You're not alone; I hear this often, that makes sense." If you want to keep the doors of communication open, it is imperative you nurture.

9. Take responsibility for everything.

10. Always help the other person preserve his/her dignity.

11. Don't be so perfect. Go for the rescue.

12. Avoid sales mouth, "The Spew"

REMEMBER:

- Everyone wants to feel OK about him/herself

- People often get their "OK'ness at the expense of other's OK'ness"

- It's a stroke-deprived world

- Always struggle intelligently on purpose

"Life is not a game of perfect."
>   *Robert J. Rotella*

"Neither is sales."
>   *PRG*

P.A.I.N./G.A.I.N.
Ground Rules
Relationship

P.A.I.N. or G.A.I.N.

Selling is a people-to-people business. Understanding people and all of their complexities:

- How they make decisions
- Why they make decisions
- How they evaluate people
- What steps they go through in the decision making process.

Having the answers to these questions are critical to being an effective salesperson. Unless you know how and why people buy, your sales results will at best, be hit or miss.

In his 1967 book, <u>The Nature of Human Intelligence</u>, J. P. Guilford defined the three separate steps that all people go through in the process of problem solving and decision-making.

Guilford defined the first step as Cognition Thinking. In this first and most important stage, we become aware of our problem or opportunity and begin to attempt to understand it. Cognition Thinking helps us realize what the problem is, understand it and ultimately move us forward in our attempt to solve it. That assumes, of course, that we determine that it is important enough to solve.

Guilford called the second stage Divergent Thinking. In this step, we begin exploring possible solutions and investigating possibilities. We then attempt to find the entire range of solutions that would best fit the situation. We develop the criteria we will use to make the best possible choice for our particular situation.

Finally, Guilford referred to the third stage as Convergent Thinking. In this stage, we apply all of the information and impressions from the first two stages to "converge" on the best possible choice.

We have taken the liberty of depicting this three-stage process in the form of a pyramidal hierarchy. Since each stage must necessarily precede the previous, a sequential hierarchy is a valid representation of this process.

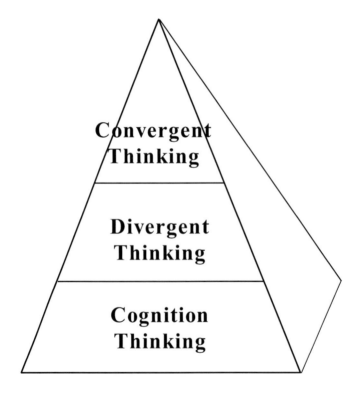

While this sequence of thinking may appear to be totally objective and devoid of any subjective, emotional input, it is anything but. From the very first stage to the last, our "emotions" guide our impressions and ultimately our opinion of what we see, hear and experience. This is the Brunswik's Lens Model, (refer back to Relationship Module) a psychological principle that advances the theory that we see, hear and feel what we want to see, hear and feel. Our opinions shape our reality and act as a filter. As a matter of fact, because our emotions play such a powerful and significant role in our lives, they can often prevent the first stage of this process, Cognition Thinking, from occurring. Instead, people can exist in states of denial or avoidance until they can get past the negative emotions associated with their situation.

The Seven Phases of the Buy-Cycle

By building upon Guilford's clinical work, we can take these thinking steps used in decision-making and further subdivide them into smaller increments. We can then discover and define the actual steps individuals and organizations use in the buying and decision-making process. Once again, we cannot over-emphasize the importance of this sequence of steps in buying since they will either help you become more effective as a seller or hamper your chances of success if you ignore them.

The seven steps or phases of the buy-cycle are, in reality, subsets of the more general descriptions identified by Guilford. These phases of buying are progressive in nature, requiring one step to be completed before the next step is initiated. This progressive order of activities can be best represented by a pyramidal hierarchy. With rare exception, each phase must be completed before the next phase can be initiated.

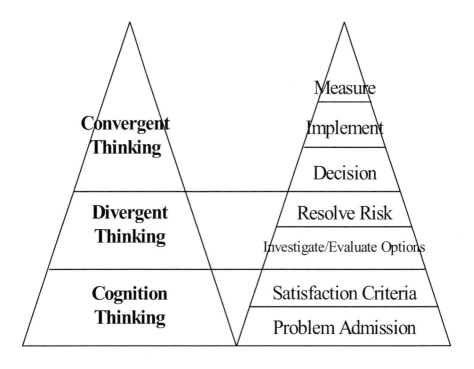

Let's look at each of the seven phases in detail and see how they relate to Guilford's steps.

Phase I of the seven-step buying process is *Problem Admission.* A buy-cycle does not begin until someone becomes dissatisfied enough with a certain situation and is willing to commit to fixing it. A problem does not get solved until someone takes ownership of it. That happens when someone initially admits that there is a problem. From the seller's perspective, it is crucial to find the person who possesses the combination of being negatively impacted by the problem and has the decision-making authority to invest resources to solve the problem. * This will be discussed in detail in the Decision Process Module.

*Power Principle:
You can only sell to someone who can buy.

Phase II of the buy-cycle is *Satisfaction Criteria.* Once an individual admits to a problem, he begins to form an idea of an alternate outcome. That is, he starts formulating a conceptual framework of what he would prefer. In this stage, the person may also begin developing pricing guidelines based upon the cost of the problem. A buyer in this phase is highly impressionable since his specifics of satisfaction are in the formulation stage. As professional salespeople, we should be willing to patiently help our potential clients develop these criteria, not through an elaborate presentation and proposal (it is far too early for that), but rather through a give-and-take exchange between both parties. This is an important step in the Discovery Selling® Process that will help him develop satisfaction criteria that will favor your solution over alternative solutions.

Phase III of the buy-cycle is *Investigation and Evaluation of Options*. At this point, the prospective client may begin speaking to other potential deliverers of the product she believes might solve the problem. She may make a number of calls to possible vendors that can supply that for which she is looking, provided that she has had limited or no contact with individuals in the particular field for which she is attempting to find a solution. If she discovers the problem by herself, or internally through another person within her facility, she will have no real loyalty or bias established to any person or for any other company.

If on the other hand, a salesperson has helped her discover the reality of her problem or situation and has spoken with her about possible solutions, chances are she is feeling a sense of comfort with and loyalty to the salesperson with whom she has that relationship (it might also be a consultant or close business associate). If the salesperson further helped her develop satisfaction criteria, a very strong bias toward that person's solutions has probably been formed in her mind. A preference has been established. In other words, once she starts looking around, her view of competitive offerings will probably be tainted by the expectations and knowledge that she and her salesperson have formulated together.

How many times have you been asked to submit a proposal for a prospect that had specifications that were clearly formulated to favor your competition? This shopping expedition usually serves to satisfy the buyer's curiosity more than anything else. Often times, however, many organizations require at least three, and possibly more price quotes. A word of caution-- avoid the mistake that many salespeople commonly make -- **THAT OF ASSUMING THE BUYER IS LOOKING FOR THE LOWEST PRICE**. If you focus primarily on price at this point, it may hurt your chances of getting the business. We'll talk more about why in the Investment Module.

Phase IV of the buy-cycle is *Resolution of Risk.* The buyer's behavior in this step can make the entire interaction up to this point come unglued if the salesperson doesn't understand the reasons behind those behaviors. The important principle to remember is that people inspect what they anticipate buying. They tend to become negative as they experience the potential risks of ownership. They start asking themselves, "What might go wrong?" The effort is directed at thinking through, and becoming comfortable with, the consequences of the decision that is about to be made. The buyer doesn't need to be sold he needs to be reassured. Aspects that increase the degree of perceived risk in the buyer's mind usually include:

- Experience with the product

- Experience with the selling organization

- Total investment

- Amount of change required

- Possible difficulties with implementation and integration

- Impact on individuals within the organization and their attitude toward that solution

- Value justification

- Personal risk tolerance

Be aware that this list is not all-inclusive and there can be many other factors, unique to each situation that will increase a buyer's perception of risk.

All of these play significant roles in creating a high or low level of perceived risk. The higher the level of risk perceived by the buyer, the greater the number of possible challenges you will have to address. One aspect of risk, the price of your product, is also one that must be resolved.

Expect most buyers to challenge it. Hearing a question along the lines of, "Is this your best price?" or "Can you do better than that on your price?" is not unusual. Notice, the buyer doesn't say he needs a lower price, he just needs to know this is the "best" you can offer. Vacillating or giving the impression that you would be willing to negotiate a lower price can actually hurt your efforts. When the buyer is ready to buy he will test your price to determine if that is the best you can do. The buyer will be ready if he knows that that's it...the price, the REAL price! Be strong in this all-important test, it's almost yours. REMEMBER, some price resistance in this phase is not only to be expected, but is also a good sign.

Exercise:

List all of the potential perceived risks of the typical buyer of your product or service. What might the buyer say to the salesperson if he/she is experiencing a particular risk?

_____

_____

_____

Phase V of the buy cycle is *Decision*. There are three possible actions that the buyer will take at this point.

1. No. "I believe it is in my best interest not to do this."

2. No decision. "There are too many things that can go wrong, it is too risky, and I am not going to decide. I will just keep thinking about it."

3. Yes. "Yes, I am doing this. It is in my best interest."

If the decision was a Yes, the buyer makes his choice and awards the business to the sales representative whom he believes can best deliver his desired solution and meet his satisfaction criteria.

Phase VI of the buy cycle is *Implementation.* In this step, the buyer, along with your assistance, implements the solution. When a buyer feels overwhelmed at the thought of implementing a solution, it can oftentimes stop the buy cycle. While some salespeople may fear that this is an objection, it should be viewed as a normal concern, which must be addressed in order for the sale to be consummated. (It may also be a real opportunity for you to differentiate yourself from the competition). Complex solutions can be potential roadblocks to the prospect moving forward. Have you ever received a commitment, thought you had the business and then realize that six months later nothing has happened? Why? Because in the customers mind, implementation was so overwhelming, they were embarrassed to ask for help or got busy with something else and nothing happened.

Phase VII of the buy-cycle is *Measurement.* Solutions, when implemented, are measured. It is those measurements that give the client the ability to determine his level of satisfaction. A buy cycle could start all over again if the client's measurement of what you deliver is deficient, based upon his expectations and your promises. To avoid this, it is important to understand his measurement criteria prior to implementation. It is the key to retaining the business once you have won it.

Taking the client's temperature, by asking him how you're performing against his expectations of you and your company, is a long-term strategy that will help make you less vulnerable to competitive attacks. Just make sure that these criteria can be measured in objective ways.

Remember this! Just because you won the business does not mean your competitors are giving up. If you are not living up to expectations, your customer might find your competitor's offerings quite intriguing and begin to initiate a new buy-cycle of which you are not aware. We'll discuss this in more depth in the Retention Module of the Discovery Selling® process.

PAIN/GAIN

Why do people buy?
What motivates people to take action?

Exercise:

List below what you believe motivates people to buy. Be general.

_____

_____

_____

Chances are, you answered the same way that most

participants answer in our live workshops. The two main

answers are:

1. They have a need.

2. They have a problem.

While both of those answers are true, they are only partially

true, as you will soon discover.

Let's explain further using an example with which you might be familiar.

Imagine for a moment that one morning, you awaken feeling a bit of pain in a tooth. It hurts enough for you to know it's there, but probably not enough for you to take action. At this point, it is not a pain; it is just a dull ache. The self-talk at this point goes something like, "I need to see a dentist. I'll call for an appointment one of these days. Maybe it will go away by itself. It's probably nothing." You now have a need...the need to see a dentist. But do you? Probably not. Most people would put it off thinking it will probably go away. This is a state, which we call either,

- Denial (it's not really anything to worry about)

- Avoidance (I know I need to do something but I'll do it later).

In any event, there's a need and maybe even a problem, but it's nothing more than an annoyance at this point so it's easy to stall and delay.

Let's take our scenario a step further. You wake up one morning, the morning of a huge presentation that, if you get the business, could make your entire annual quota with one order. You've prepared for weeks, and know that you can, and more than likely will, win the business. It's going to be a great day! However, you take a sip of cold orange juice and when the chill of the beverage hits that pesky tooth; it's like a lightning bolt hitting your brain. You grimace with pain. Bracing yourself at your kitchen counter, you wait for the throbbing to subside, but it doesn't. In fact, it gets worse. Within an hour you are in complete agony. The pain is unbearable. What do you do? What any sane individual would do. Get on the phone immediately to make an emergency appointment with your dentist or with any dentist who will see you. Your need, your problem, has now become a pain. What made it so? Physical discomfort yes, but also the dreaded thought of possibly not being able to deliver the presentation you have been anticipating for so long. You are now deeply impacted by the need/problem due to its consequences. *Question*: What are you **not** thinking at this point? *Answer*: How much will it cost? Your efforts are directed at one thing and one thing only, ending the pain as quickly as possible. You have become a solid prospect for the dentist who can:

1. See you immediately
2. Stop the pain.

You have begun a buy-cycle.

Why do some people bog down in a morass of indecision while others are decisive and act quickly? The concepts of

P.A.I.N. and G.A.I.N. are the reasons. Understanding this concept and its profound implications to sales success can help you become a world-class, gold medal seller.

The basis of almost all actions that we as human beings take is motivated by one of two similar forces. The reasons that we take action in almost everything we do is the need to avoid or eliminate P.A.I.N. or the desire to G.A.I.N. or achieve something extremely important. These forces create powerful emotions within each of us that will cause us to be motivated to act. Sigmund Freud, the father of modern psychology, stated that emotions control our lives. With this in mind we must understand that we are calling on "people" when we are interacting with prospective customers…PEOPLE. When you fully grasp this concept, you can then begin to understand why so many sales efforts are unsuccessful.

When you approach a potential customer and hear her explain a few surface- level needs, and then rush to a proposal, presentation or a demo stressing your features and benefits, you are selling at an intellectual level only. Can you be successful? The answer is maybe. In a small percentage of the cases where the P.A.I.N. is so great and has already been admitted by the prospective customer with whom you are speaking and that person can see the end of her distress by buying what you offer, the chances of success are very good. However, that only happens sometimes. That's why some sales are very easy, while others are far more difficult, time-consuming and less successful. In the case of the latter, more often than not, the P.A.I.N. has not been admitted or fully understood. Think back to the toothache example we used as our illustration. How much selling did the dentist have to do when you were in a high level of P.A.I.N.? Probably very little. What you wanted more than anything, at that point was for the dentist to "understand your situation" and end the hurt. Move back a step further and think about your feelings before the P.A.I.N. was severe. If a dentist had made a "sales call" (it even sounds silly) on you, stressing the friendliness of his staff, the cleanliness of his office, the marvelous pricing policies he had in place, and the depth of his education, would you have automatically bought? Probably not. While all of those are important aspects of a professional dental practice, they really did not matter to you at that point because you didn't really feel you needed them. If, on the other hand, he had carried it a step further and helped you understand the impact of the "tooth problem" you had, as well as the consequences of not taking action quickly to stave off the dire outcome, you would have been more likely to decide on a course of action.

So, to state it again, these powerful emotional energies that we call P.A.I.N. and G.A.I.N. are the gasoline that powers our behavioral engines. Logic alone is almost never enough to cause action. Knowing and understanding this profound insight will help you gain a strong competitive advantage in your marketplace.

Power Principle:
People make emotional decisions for logical reasons. The two most powerful emotions are P.A.I.N. and G.A.I.N.

Exercise:

To illustrate this point please complete the following exercise: Find any nationally distributed magazine, TIME, Newsweek, Cosmopolitan, Oprah, Sports Illustrated, etc.

Thumb through the ads and notice whether they appeal to your senses (emotions) or to your intellect (logic). Clip out the most compelling ad and decide to which emotion it appeals.

You may also notice that the most effective TV ads are those that appeal to your emotions (generally the large budget national advertisers), while the majority of local ads attempt to appeal to your intellect. Now, find one of those obnoxious local TV ads that really annoy you. Does it attempt to appeal to your emotions or to your intellect? Chances are that they are trying to get you excited by their delivery (screaming and yelling and acting very excited and enthusiastic). It usually has the opposite affect. The ads, which have the greatest effectiveness, are the ones targeted at your emotions, while the ones that tend to be most objectionable are those targeting your intellect.

So, we salespeople should learn from the Madison Avenue crowd. They appeal to your emotions, not to your logic. They know that if they can get you to really want something by appealing to your emotions, you will come up with all of the logical reasons that you should have it. Let's deal with emotions first when we sell, and logic second.

Let's repeat the definition of selling:

> Selling is the art and science of helping people discover that which is in their best interest by helping them get in touch with what's important to them at a personal, emotional level.

One of the most important elements of that definition is *"by helping them get in touch with what's most important to them at a personal, emotional level."*

People ALWAYS do what they perceive to be in their own best interest. The way they arrive at this conclusion is through their highly "subjective" and prejudicial "emotional" filter. With the decision thus made, they then go about gathering the required supporting data to justify that highly emotional decision. This is the theory behind Brunswik's Lens Model of Reality (which is anything but). This concept will be further explained through the science of Transactional Analysis in the Understanding Human Interactions Module.

P.A.I.N. Definition

Now that you have a basic understanding of these twin forces of P.A.I.N./G.A.I.N., let's look at the definitions of each that will help you understand how to apply them to the selling process.

P.A.I.N. is a person's personal, emotional involvement with their problem or situation.

G.A.I.N. is the P.A.I.N. of not having something. The dictionary uses the word *distress* to define P.A.I.N., and that's a good word to keep in mind as we seek to understand it. Distress can be physical or it can be mental.

While we have elaborated on the concept of P.A.I.N., it is also important to understand G.A.I.N. and the subtle differences between the two.

Have you ever personally wanted something? Perhaps it was a goal or you wanted to own something. Your heart was set on it and mentally you decided that you just had to have it. But, in the end, it didn't happen. You didn't get it. Did it hurt? Did you feel bad? Did you feel like you had lost something extremely important? Were you upset? That was G.A.I.N. The overwhelming desire to have something and the inability to get it causes emotional distress and that's G.A.I.N. While you survived without it, the feeling of disappointment was unpleasant and probably one you would have preferred to avoid. That's how G.A.I.N. is actually a P.A.I.N. It is the future brought into the present. For purposes of our discussions, from this point forward, we will refer to the entire range of emotions, as it relates to this concept simply as P.A.I.N.

As human beings we are all different. As you have discovered in previous chapters, all people think differently. Some of us think only in the present and seldom look into the future. This group tends to be *reactive* in nature usually waiting until trouble strikes before taking any action. This group will typically avoid taking preventive actions to stop a real problem before it starts.

Others tend to think more into the future. This group is *proactive* in nature and usually takes action in advance of trouble. Both groups may deal with a similar problem, but have very dissimilar timetables. Some wait, some act.

P.A.I.N. Expanded

P.A.I.N. is the gap between expectation and reality. Let's use your car as an example. You might be quite satisfied with it right now. But, over the course of time, it will begin to show signs of aging. It will need repairs, some of which can be costly. It may become less dependable or it might not portray the "right kind of image" you need in your particular line of work. Your satisfaction with your vehicle, however you may define it, will decrease while your dissatisfaction with it will increase over time. At some point, the gap between satisfaction and dissatisfaction will be great enough for you to say, "That's it, time for a new car!" At this point, you are motivated by P.A.I.N. ("I'm spending too much") or G.A.I.N. ("I love this new car, I deserve it"). That's when you become a serious prospect to one or several automobile dealerships. Prior to that gap, no amount of convincing, closing, pressure, presenting, pitching or objection handling would make you a prospect. You decided when you were ready for a new car, not an aggressive salesperson.

P.A.I.N. Is Pre-Existing

We're often asked, "How do I create P.A.I.N.?" The answer is, YOU DON'T! You uncover it. It's there before you or any salesperson shows up. The goal is to get the P.A.I.N. on the table for a discussion. The Discovery Selling® process is oriented to bring P.A.I.N. to the surface. That helps the buyer develop an awareness and even an understanding of the gap that may accelerate his/her dissatisfaction to the point of becoming a prospect and ultimately a client or customer.

Power Principle:
The prospect must discover his P.A.I.N. You cannot tell him he has it.

Exercise:

What might be the prospects reaction when you attempt to

TELL him he has a problem? Write down your answers

below.

_____

_____

_____

_____

When you attempt to tell or convince a potential customer

that he has P.A.I.N., (in essence trying to create it) you can

expect one of two common reactions:

- It will almost assuredly push the person into a state
  of denial. The prospect will do everything in his
  power to convince you that he has no problems at all
  and that everything is just wonderful. He might even
  be courteous enough to ask you for a brochure and
  encourage you to stop by and see him next time
  you're in the area. NO PROSPECT THERE. There

is also the possibility that the prospect might be offended at your crass attempt to be so bold as to suggest that he has, heaven forbid, any problems. Though he might not say that to you, and will act courteous in spite of it, he will get rid of you as quickly as possible. The best way for him to do that is to act interested and to request some additional information. He will then avoid talking with you in the future (not a strong relationship-building strategy).

- The second predictable reaction to trying to tell someone that they have a problem is one of avoidance. The prospect may indeed admit a "minor" problem, but then tell you all of the reasons that it cannot be addressed presently. He'll then show great interest in your offerings, as in the first example, and will probably suggest that he'll get back in touch with you at some unspecified future date. This interest, of course, gets you excited enough to "buy the lie" and you scurry on your merry little way thinking you've found a new prospect. NOT! Prospects learned long ago that if they acted really, really interested and very positive, they could get rid of almost any salesperson they encountered. So, this display of Optimism and Enthusiasm is your ticket to the prospect's voice mail system. It's over in his mind, but the beginning of something wonderful in yours. *

*Power Principle:
You don't have a prospect until there is admitted P.A.I.N. accompanied by a commitment.

The Importance of Buyer Orientation

By now the differences in the traditional approach to selling and the Discovery Selling® approach should be obvious.

The standard sales methodology focuses on the salesperson and strategies to control the buyer. The traditional methods stress using a features and benefits approach to selling. It presumes that the buyer will be so impressed with their value that he will undoubtedly see the error of his ways and buy what you are offering. Traditional selling held the belief that we salespeople had to educate our prospects.

In reality, this type of selling is, in a very subtle and unspoken way, sending the wrong message. In essence, this methodology is saying: "Hey stupid, can't you figure it out? How could you possibly not buy from me? Are you an idiot? What's wrong with you?"

It is hard to imagine that this was ever the intent of the salesperson, but the message came through loud and clear, nevertheless. The salesperson made the buyer feel stupid, ignorant or incompetent, and then couldn't understand why he faced such strong resistance to his offerings. When your prospect sees you as an ally, not as a salesperson, your chances of success increase by <u>huge proportions.</u>

When you master and discipline yourself to apply The Discovery Selling® process, it will actually help you work with your prospects in ways that foster trust, honesty, and respect. It will help you truly understand the buyer and guide you along a pathway that will enhance the relationship, not detract from it. The buyer must always feel that he is in control. The more he feels in control, the more likely he is to cooperate with you as you seek to help him take appropriate action that truly serve his best interests.

Forget the Techniques

Techniques can be very harmful to building relationships, particularly in their early, formative stages. The old techniques that have been around for decades are usually recognized by most buyers and scream of insincerity. They send a signal to the person that he must keep his guard up. The source of most buyer/seller tension can be traced to the use of techniques that the buyer recognizes. His way of fighting back is to become resistant. These over-used, outdated techniques, which are unfortunately still being taught to and used by some salespeople, are best left where they are found; in the one-day seminars and within the pages of the "silver bullet" sales books. Be a *real person* and have *real conversations* with your prospects, who are after all *real people* with *real feelings*, and you'll find that they will, more often than not, respond in kind. *

When your behavior, not just your words, convey the message that you are truly trying to help, and only want the prospect to do what she perceives to be in her best interest, it opens a whole new world of opportunities for both of you.

*Power Principle:
Your intentions are more important than your techniques.

Orienting Yourself with the Buyer

As has been mentioned earlier, professional selling is doing the right thing at the right time in the right way. It is critical. Let's use closing as an example since so much is made of it. Salespeople, because of that thing called a "quota"; rush to close the business long before it is closeable. When they do that, it hurts the relationship they have worked so hard to build. This action ultimately reduces the level of trust. The message that premature closing sends to the buyer is, "I'm doing what's best for me, not you!"

On the other hand, closing at the right time, in the right way is an effortless activity. In fact, it is our observation, as well as that of many other top salespeople, when the business is closeable all the salesperson need do is facilitate the close. It becomes virtually effortless. The old adage, close early, close often, is great advice for salespeople who want to get only one order. The goal of Discover Selling® is to help you develop an ongoing business relationship that has value for both buyer and seller. That will take more time, and when it's time to close, it will happen very naturally.

Remember this, when the prospect says "yes" and buys, it is seldom the first "yes" he has given to you. The order is just another "yes" in a sequence of "yeses". The way to get to that point is best accomplished by orienting your activities to the prospect's buying phase. This will help you utilize the appropriate selling behavior. It will enhance the relationship, actually speed up his progress through the phases, and foster increased buyer satisfaction.

The reason we address this all-important issue at this point serves a very solid purpose. When you as a salesperson commit to helping your prospects *admit* P.A.I.N., you will find that he will typically share his problems with you rather quickly. It is a real temptation to pounce on problems and start "selling" by presenting solutions. This is usually a big mistake. The reason is because you will have shifted roles from that of an ally into that of a salesperson. The prospect will feel tricked, manipulated, and taken advantage of, if that occurs. It will predictably do great harm to a relationship in any stage of its development. In fact, it will usually kill it! You must resist your urge to start presenting by making a personal commitment to go all of the way through the Discovery Selling® process (remember the Guilford Model and the Seven Phases of the Buy-Cycle). If you will be disciplined about following the Discovery Selling® process, you'll be rewarded with significantly improved outcomes.

Power Principle:
The best way to be an effective seller is by being a facilitator of the buying process.

Modes of P.A.I.N.

When prospects experience P.A.I.N., it can be in one of three possible modes.

Mode I: P.A.I.N. in the present. This describes the prospect that has already discovered a problem, understands the impact of the problem on herself and the organization, and is highly motivated to take action quickly. In this mode, trouble has occurred or is occurring at the present time and the prospect wants it to be stopped. This describes every salesperson's ideal prospect. That's the one we are all seeking, but it also represents a small number of potential buyers.

Prospects in high levels of P.A.I.N. usually initiate contact in an attempt to find a solution. It is reasonable to assume that any prospect in a dire situation in the present is ready to make a buying decision if she sees an end to the problem with your solution. It would be nice if all prospects we meet with were in this mode, but unfortunately they are not. There are certainly not enough pre-existing Mode I prospects to achieve our sales goals. Typically, in our workshops, when we ask how many prospects in a specific market area or territory fit the Mode I criteria, we hear a range of between 5-15%. Indeed, if we're not already talking to them, we soon will be.

The remaining group of potential customers, who could and would be qualified for what we sell and have a need, are in either Mode II or Mode III, both of which are future-based, unlike Mode I which is in the present.

Mode II: P.A.I.N. is coming. Mode II describes the prospect who anticipates problems coming. This is a fear-based mode; that being the fear of impending negative consequences if preventive action is not taken. Because this is a future-based time frame, it is a lot easier for the prospect to delay taking action, or moving into a state of avoidance. The salesperson's primary goal with a Mode II prospect is to bring the future into the present by helping the person understand the implications and consequences of inaction.

A word of caution here is in order. Go slowly. Do not threaten and do not push too hard. Softly and gently, you must help the prospect see the reality of his situation. This is accomplished through the questioning skills that you will learn about in the **Questions Are The Answer** module. The insurance industry sells to Mode II prospects. You don't buy insurance because you need it right now (usually if you do, they won't sell it to you), but because of fear that something bad might happen.

Mode III: G.A.I.N. Mode III describes those who are trying to achieve something in the future and it is extremely important, even critical, that it be achieved. They are motivated by a vision or a goal that creates a strong and overpowering desire. In this mode, the prospect admits the desire. The implications and feelings of not achieving the goal or acquiring the desired outcome is the P.A.I.N. associated with Mode III. The salesperson's goal with a Mode III prospect is to help them admit the potential roadblocks to success and feel the P.A.I.N. of not achieving the goal. That brings the future into the present, makes it a P.A.I.N., and facilitates the selling process much more effectively.

The P.A.I.N./G.A.I.N. Acronyms

You'll notice throughout this section, we have referred to P.A.I.N./G.A.I.N. as acronyms. We do this so that you will begin thinking of these two concepts in the appropriate ways. Each of the letters of **P.A.I.N.** and **G.A.I.N.** represent a word that relates to its meaning.

P. problems, prevention

A. aggravations, apprehensions

I. irritations

N. negative feelings

G. goals, growth

A. achievement, acquire

I. improvement, increase

N. new insights

Exercise:

Using the letters in the acronyms **P.A.I.N./G.A.I.N.**, list any other words that would fit the description of **P.A.I.N./G.A.I.N.**?

P. _____   G. _____
A. _____   A. _____
I. _____   I. _____
N. _____   N. _____

The Four Levels of P.A.I.N./G.A.I.N.

When we begin an interaction with any prospect, the salesperson's goal is to qualify the prospect, and then align his activities to fit the prospect's place in the buy-cycle.

Before we explain how to do that, you must first understand the four specific levels of P.A.I.N. through which a prospect goes. We have touched on each of them briefly and have chosen to illustrate them with a pyramidal hierarchy, as we have done with other key concepts. The four levels of P.A.I.N. are shown in the following illustration.

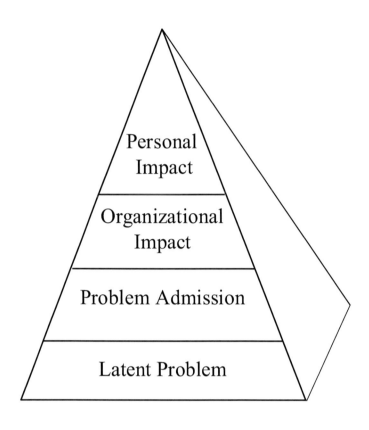

Level I. Latent P.A.I.N. Prospects who do not have an admitted problem are said to be in latent P.A.I.N. A prospect in **P.A.I.N. Level One** needs help and encouragement to admit that there is a problem. Perhaps it is a problem of which they are unaware. By asking a question such as, "What issues would you be attempting to address?" may help uncover surface problems. That may sound like a rather simplistic question to you, however do not underestimate its power. If the prospect doesn't have any answers, you can suggest some issues that might be worthy of addressing. If the prospect does have some answers, write them down. That's the beginning of P.A.I.N.

Level II. Admit P.A.I.N. Sometimes the prospect will volunteer, almost immediately, their problems, frustrations, or concerns. Sometimes this will surface in the Accomplish step of the Ground Rules. If they do volunteer information, write them down. Get a list. Be patient and ask, "Is there anything else?" or "What else?" Don't move too quickly. Be certain you get a complete list. Remember there is almost always more than just one problem. Move slowly and, for heaven's sake, DO NOT START SELLING!

Level III. Organizational Impact. Problems within any organization seldom affect only one department or one individual. Therefore, in this step, we are seeking to find out how far the stated problem reaches and its broader implications. The wider the reach the more costly the problem becomes, thus creating greater negative consequences. In this stage of P.A.I.N. discovery, consider asking several the following questions:

- "How does this affect your department?"
- "How does this affect your organization?'
- "Who else is affected by this problem?"
- "How has this affected the bottom line?"

Don't be surprised if the person to whom you are speaking does not know. That's your chance to ask, "Who would know?" and provides you with at least a valid reason for needing to speak to that person who does know, and who is also, no doubt, impacted by the problem. It will help you understand the cost associated with the problem, by doing a thorough job of information gathering in this stage. That will usually go a long way to supporting your value justification. Problems cost money. The cost of the solution will always be measured against the cost of the problem. That is the measure of value and places your price in the proper context. *Warning*: DO NOT START SELLING.

Level IV. Personal Impact. Organizations have problems. Problems affect people. Personal impact describes how any given individual to whom you speak, regarding the problem, might be personally affected by that problem. Once a person expresses, at a feeling level, the impact that the problem is having on either their personal or professional life, you have found P.A.I.N. You needn't dig any deeper. Warning: DO NOT START SELLING!

How To Find P.A.I.N.

Most salespeople say that the hardest part of a sales call is the beginning. Through the use of the Ground Rules format, you will find that beginning any sales call will be much easier. By simply asking the "Accomplish" question, which you can do if you did an effective job on the phone when you set the appointment, you'll begin hearing basic level issues almost immediately. The prospect will normally open up.

"But," you ask, "what if I don't have an appointment? I can't ask the "Accomplish" question so what should I do?" That's a valid point and requires a different approach.

Perhaps you just stopped in and luckily* were invited in to speak to someone. You will still follow the Ground Rules sequence. When you come to the Accomplish step, instead of asking, "What would you like to accomplish", suggest some initial surface issues that might be the focal point for your interaction. Do not go into product descriptions, corporate strategies or features and benefits diatribes. The prospect doesn't care and it might keep the conversation from going toward a meaningful direction.

Instead, you might say something such as,

"As you know, I represent _____ (insert company name). We work with a variety of organizations to help them address some of the frustrations they may be having with their_____ (insert generic problems you and your company address. Keep it more global in nature). Typically, they tell us that they have concerns in one of several areas. Some are trying to_____ (insert specific P/A.I.N you/your company can solve. Others are attempting to improve _____ (insert other P.A.I.N you can solve). Still others are having difficulty with _____ (insert

additional P.A.I.N). So that we can invest our time on the area that is most important to you, which of those areas seems to be causing you the greatest concern?"

That will usually give the prospect the opportunity to select the topic most important to him. He may say that none of them are important. Consequently, he may tell you about an alternate issue. However, if the prospect doesn't select one of the issues that you mentioned and doesn't volunteer an alternate issue, then you can ask a follow-up question such as:

"In my experience, there typically is one area where something should be occurring in your organization in the area of _____ that is not. If you had to pick one area in which you are not achieving the results you need, what would that be?

This is similar to the question you might ask of a prospect with latent P.A.I.N. Remember, you must get them to admit a problem or a concern.

*Power Principle:
Luck is preparation, meeting opportunity.

There are countless other ways to initiate this buyer/seller conversation and space prohibits listing them all. The important point to remember is there has to be an admitted problem and you must understand what that problem is and develop it into P.A.I.N. Typically, you and your product or service address the same four or five pains. Your job is to ask the right questions to help your prospect discover the issues that are most important to him.

This strategy is one for which you must prepare. Don't try to wing it. Once you have it down and are fully prepared, you will not fall victim to the prospect who says, "I don't have much time. I'll give you five minutes. Tell me, what can you do for us?"

Your answer in this scenario should always be the same.

Memorize it.

> *"At this point, I'm not really sure what we might be able to do. Would it be alright if I asked you a few questions to get a better understanding of your current situation so that I would be able to answer that question intelligently?"*

Pay attention to your tone of voice when you say this.

Speak softly and slowly because you are seeking

permission. *

*Power Principle:
You don't qualify a prospect by talking, you qualify by listening.

Once you've made it past the initial difficulty that you may

encounter in the opening moments of a sales call, follow

the sequence through the levels of P.A.I.N. After you've

done this, your prospect will usually be eager to find out

how you might be able to help.

Exercise:

Assume you have asked the following question: "What issues would you be attempting to address if you used (*insert your product or service)* within your organization?" Write down a likely response that you might hear in each Mode.

P.A.I.N. Mode I

_____
_____
_____
_____

P.A.I.N. Mode II (Fear)

_____
_____
_____
_____

G.A.I.N. Mode III (Goals)

_____
_____
_____
_____

Exercise:

For each of the following four levels of P.A.I.N., create at least four questions that will help you gather further insight into the existing situation for that prospect and his organization.

Level I—Latent P.A.I.N

_____

_____

_____

_____

Level II—Admit P.A.I.N.

_____

_____

_____

_____

Level III—Impact on the Organization

_____

_____

_____

_____

Level IV—Personal Impact

_____

_____

_____

_____

Creating the above questions will help you prepare for the

process of discovering P.A.I.N. You may also utilize this

information to prospect for new customers.

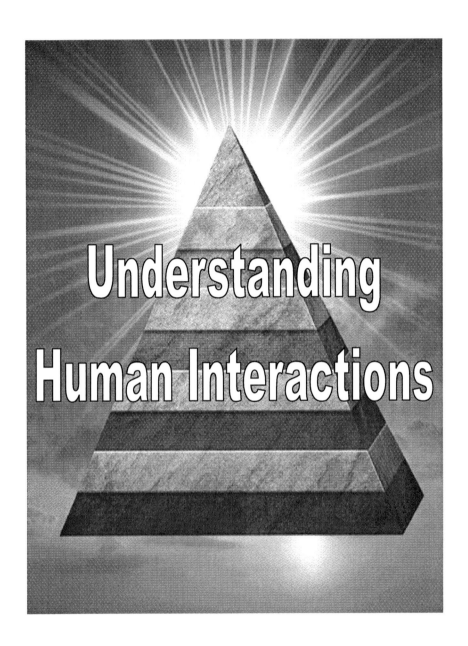

Understanding Human Interactions

Understanding Human Interactions:
The Key to Effective Selling

P.A.I.N. discovery is one of the more difficult selling tasks faced, because it requires a great deal of patience on the salesperson's part and because it tends to make the prospect feel vulnerable. In order for a person to share his P.A.I.N., he must feel that he is in a non-threatening environment and that the salesperson will not abuse or misuse the information he shares. The prospect realizes that once he admits his P.A.I.N., he is literally at the salesperson's mercy. This realization, even at a subconscious level, keeps the prospect from sharing information. Therefore, it is mandatory that a salesperson position himself in a non-threatening manner that makes it safe for the prospect to share information. Some background information on psychological principles as they relate to the communication process will be helpful to the salesperson in creating that safe environment.

In reality, communication is the lowest common denominator to being effective as a salesperson. As you have already learned, people buy emotionally and the ability of a salesperson to find P.A.I.N., though effective communication is a skill that must be developed. The principles of Transactional Analysis lend themselves to aiding the salesperson in developing the necessary skills to allow him to proceed through the sales process in a non-threatening manner and will enable him to find out the "real issues" the prospect is facing.

What is Transactional Analysis?

Transactional Analysis, or T-A, is a way of observing and measuring the interactions between people (overtly). T-A also helps in understanding what emotions and thinking processes go on inside people (covertly). This understanding lends itself to explaining human situations that occur daily and will foster insight into understanding common, everyday interactions. The ultimate objective in using Transactional Analysis is to help people become aware of unproductive human interactions and experiences. This awareness will assist willing parties in changing behaviors so that every interaction becomes win/win.

Discovery Selling® uses the theories of Transactional Analysis to describe interactions, actions, and reactions in a selling situation (transactions), and to help each encounter end with an optimum result. Ideally, people must learn to monitor their sales encounters and learn to adjust their behavior so that every sales interaction results in a win/win.

Transactional Analysis Concepts

The major concept of Transactional Analysis that we as salespeople need to understand is that of Ego States (discussed in more detail on the following pages). As is true for every person, our own Ego States reveal themselves to us through a constantly occurring and a constantly changing stream of self-talk.

This self-talk is sometimes in the form of an argument, sometimes in the form of a discussion, sometimes in the form of a scolding, and sometimes in the form of praise. Whatever the self-talk is, it springs from an Ego State. What we say or do at a particular time is very much influenced by whatever self-talk is simultaneously occurring. These various inner discussions determine our attitude about any given situation and they reveal themselves to the world through our spoken words and our observable actions and behaviors.

Just as Ego States influence us as salespeople, they influence our customers. By knowing more about this fascinating subject, you can better understand what may be going on in the mind of your customer (wouldn't that be nice?) simply by listening and observing. Also you can better understand the importance your own Ego State plays in creating a positive sales outcome.

T-A theorizes that all interactions are comprised of strokes and transactions that are derived from our Ego States. A STROKE is any form of recognition, either positive or negative. A TRANSACTION is an exchange of strokes between two people. The first stroke is called a stimulus and the second stroke is called a response.

Power Principle:
Choosing how you respond to a stimulus will enable you to effectively communicate.

How might choosing your response be in your best interest?

_____

_____

_____

_____

How might choosing your response be in the prospect's interest?

_____

_____

_____

_____

EGO STATES

Inside every human being, there resides three major Ego States: The Parent Ego State, the Adult Ego State, and the Child Ego State. Let's examine each one for understanding.

The Parent Ego State

The Parent Ego State begins forming at birth and continues forming until age 6 or 7. This Ego State records information, much like a video camera. It begins recording at birth. It records all you see and hear from those around you. It records all external events that occur. All of your rules, opinions, and prejudices are formed at this time and stored in your Parent Ego State. The child receiving these messages records them as *truth*. Your Parent Ego State also records your thoughts about events and activities. At this stage, most of your interactions are with your parents (or those playing a parental role); therefore most of your scripts are received and recorded directly from the parents. However scripting can occur from *any person* a child perceives to be an authority figure. All data is received without editing. It is accepted at face value. The tapes that are recorded can play back at any time during our lives, oftentimes at a subconscious level. Because they cause automatic or reflexive reactions, they can be triggered at any time. Like pushing the "play" button on a VCR (stimulus), the tape starts playing (response) automatically.

The Parent Ego state is our source of praise and protection and is made up of two components.

> **Nurturing Parent:** The Nurturing Parent Ego State is loving and nurturing. We get our positive strokes from this Ego State. The Nurturing Parent

always makes the wounded child feel better. A wounded child will seek the nurturing parent when he is hurting, either physically or psychologically. In addition, children seek the attention and approval of the Nurturing Parent to remain psychologically OK because the Nurturing Parent enhances self-esteem. Watch little children asking a parent to "Watch me do this." They seek the strokes that the Nurturing Parent can provide.

Critical Parent: The Critical Parent Ego State is critical and judgmental, and reprimands a disobedient child. This Parental Ego State is the finger pointer. This is the component that says, "You **should** have done this, or you **should** have done that…etc." More than just a disciplinarian in childhood, the Critical Parent is the protector. The Critical Parent helps us stay safe by teaching us the rules, such as, "Look both ways before crossing a street, Don't talk to strangers, etc."

The Child Ego State

The Child Ego State begins recording information at birth and continues development until age 6 or 7. It too, is like a video camera. Unlike the Parent that records external events, the Child records all internal events through its experiences. Both the Parent and the Child are recording simultaneously. The recordings the Child makes are all of the responses he *feels* while the external events are occurring. Therefore, all of one's emotions reside in the Child Ego State. Emotions such as: scared, mad, sad, and glad. It is the "feelings" ego state. When a person is emotional, the Child Ego State has taken control. The Child Ego State has the ability to rapidly cascade between feelings. You can observe this quite readily in a little child who will be crying about something one moment, and immediately turns to laughter the next.

The Child ego state is comprised of several components:

Natural Child: The Natural Child Ego State is the fun-loving, free spirited part of us. It represents our creativity as well as our rebelliousness. It is the part of a person that sets no limits, is completely self-centered and cares only about him or herself. The important point to remember is that the person in a Natural Child Ego State is emotionally out of control. The Natural Child Ego State has three subcomponents.

1. *The Rebel*: This is the ego state that does the exact opposite of what you want them to do. If you say Up, they'll say Down, if you say Black, they'll say White. Think of teenagers and you'll fully understand the rebellious child. They fight the parent constantly, rebelling against rules, particularly the Critical Parent. When a prospect begins hammering you with objections, could it be as a result of triggering his

Rebellious Child by you acting or sounding like a Critical Parent? Could presenting solutions too early sound like you are being critical? Watch the prospect's reaction for the answer.

2. *The Wounded Child*: This is the ego state that contains hurt feelings. As an adult, if the Wounded Child feels threatened, he may rapidly revert to the Rebellious Child Ego State to protect himself. The Rebellious Child will automatically fight, and then usually cascade to the Critical Parent as his means of protection. In a sales call, if the prospect feels safe he will share his P.A.I.N., however if at any time he feels threatened while sharing his P.A.I.N. he reverts to either the Critical Parent or Rebellious Child and go on the attack.

3. *The Playful Child*: This is the ego state that likes to have fun. Curiosity and creativity reside in the Playful Child. On a sales call, these attributes can

sometimes get you into trouble. Sometimes, the Playful Child will take over at inappropriate times and may cause an adverse reaction from the prospect. An example of this may be telling an off-color joke. The Playful Child may affect your judgment, causing you to act inappropriately.

Adapted Child: In this Ego State, we adapt our behavior to receive "mother's love". We learn that when an authority figure gives approval, it makes us feel good inside. Therefore, we do things, say things, and act in certain ways to receive approval, i.e. Strokes.

In sales, the Adapted Child Ego State can be a major hindrance and will cause us difficulty when it is time to close a sale, since we seek approval from the parent (prospect) rather than the order. Salespeople with a strong Adapted Child fear the loss of approval of a prospect. That makes for a reward/punishment type of relationship, rather than a productive ongoing business relationship.

Little Professor: The Little Professor is the ego state that has figured out how to get strokes. He/she does this by letting others know how smart he/she is. Small children like to tell you things that they have learned to receive recognition from adults.

As salespeople, we will sometimes go in and "spew" information to let the prospect know how much we know. Unfortunately, the Little Professor often does this prior to determining the important issues the prospect is facing. At a subconscious level, we do this to receive strokes.

Power Principle:
Sales is a profession to meet your financial needs, not your emotional needs.

The Adult Ego State

The Adult Ego state begins at approximately ten months

and continues throughout your life. It doesn't record, it

observes. It is detached. It is similar to a computer—it only analyzes information. Information in, information out. The Adult Ego State is logical, non-emotional, and analytical. It has no opinions. The Adult Ego State is continually asking: who, what, when, where, and why. It is continually analyzing what is different about life from the concepts taught by the Parent, and the feelings concepts of the Child. Therefore, as information is accumulated, the Adult will receive information, compute whether that information is still appropriate, and then respond in a logical manner. The Adult is capable of computing consequences. A good example of an Adult Ego State (although overextended) is Mr. Spock on Star Trek. He is totally unemotional, logical, and analytical. Feelings and opinions never enter into the Adult's thought process. It is purely analytical. Because of this, people with a very strong Adult Ego State can be seen as un-caring, ambivalent, and indifferent.

T-A On A Sales Call

There is no place for the Child Ego State or the Critical Parent Ego State in your selling. In reality, you should be in the Adult Ego State at all times. You should, however, *act* as a nurturing parent 75% of the time and *act* as adult 25% of the time. Do not be condescending or overly analytical –empathize. Give appropriate strokes when you can and avoid becoming a victim of a stimulus that could cause you to react from your Child Ego State. You do have a choice. There is no place for emotions on a sales call.

Power Principle:
People buy emotionally and justify intellectually.

TRANSACTIONS

When you communicate with others you will be doing it from one of the three main ego states. There are two types of transactions, *complementary* and *crossed*.

A *complementary transaction* occurs when two people are communicating in parallel ego states, for example, Parent-to-Parent, Adult-to-Adult, Child-to-Child, etc.

```
P  ←――――――――→  P
A  ←――――――――→  A
C  ←――――――――→  C
```

Complementary Transactions

A Parent-to-Parent transaction is the sharing of opinions.

An Adult-to-Adult transaction is the sharing of information.

A Child-to-Child transaction is the sharing of emotional

experiences. A Parent-to-Child transaction may be that of an authority figure helping another with an emotional need.

Another type of transaction is a *crossed transaction*. A crossed transaction is when stimulus and response get crossed in the PAC transactional diagram. This occurs when one moves through the ego states very quickly during a conversation. A crossed transaction will cause trouble and stop communication. Whenever there is a crossed transaction there is a breakdown in communication and true communication stops.

Author's Note:

> *"My husband came into the kitchen one morning and asked, 'Where are my running shorts?' I told him that they were in his bottom drawer. He said, 'I already looked and they are not there'. I then said, 'Did you move things around to try to find them?' He then told me he did and could not find them. I then went and found them for him. At this point we were both aggravated at each other and in a matter*

of seconds this conversation had turned into an argument. We just had a crossed transaction. The conversation started as an Adult-to-Adult interaction. He asked me 'Where are my shorts?' and I said 'In your bottom drawer.' When he replied with a surly tone, 'I already looked and they are not in there' he moved to a Child Ego State. He became emotional. I then moved to the Critical Parent Ego State by saying 'Did you move things around to try to find them?' (more critical).

As you can tell from this conversation, one can move or cascade through these ego states very quickly and at a subconscious level. The original focus of the conversation (finding the shorts) was completely lost and the new focus became 'being right", which resulted in an argument. Communication stopped. We could no longer discuss his running shorts and the conversation turned to his inability to find things. That issue had to be resolved first before productive communication could resume.

Obviously, crossed transactions should be avoided. A clearer understanding of the Ego States will enable you to recognize that between every stimulus and response there is a gap. It is within the gap, that you can choose how to respond.

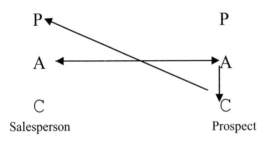

Crossed Transaction

Application

Discovery Selling® was designed to help you maintain open communication through the use of complementary transactions. Learn to recognize your Child along with its vulnerabilities. Learn to recognize and be sensitive to your prospect's Child. Learn to stroke and protect the prospect's

Child. Be aware of your Parent and watch how you position your words. Watch your tonality and body language. Make sure you are Nurturing and not Critical. The Critical Parent will cause a crossed transaction.

Note: Our objective in communicating is to have parallel transactions that are complementary and maintain the flow of information.

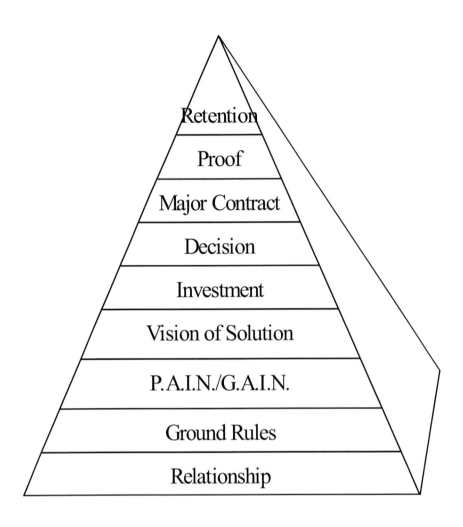

Relationship

Relationship is based upon trust. Trust is achieved through Sincerity, Honesty, and Competence. This is done through matching and mirroring the prospect. You match and mirror through body language, tone, and words. This will create a comfort level and set the stage for an Adult-to-Adult transaction.

Ground Rules

Ground Rules is an Adult-to-Adult transaction. If you will recall, the Adult Ego State is analytical and asks the questions who, what, when, where, why and how. When laying the Ground Rules, both parties mutually commit to the time frame of the meeting and to what will specifically occur at the meeting. A very important component of Ground Rules is getting permission to ask questions. This opens the door for the next level of the Qualification Pyramid.

P.A.I.N. / GA.I.N.

P.A.I.N. is obviously an emotion that we are attempting to uncover. This particular emotion occurs in the Wounded Child State. The only way to find P.A.I.N. is to create a non-threatening environment (accomplished in the Ground Rules step) and to ask questions. To be truly effective, you must ask the right questions the right way at the right time. In the P.A.I.N. / G.A.I.N. step, the salesperson needs to move into the Nurturing Parent role. If you will recall, the Nurturing Parent always is comforting to the Wounded Child and is a source of strokes. The Nurturing Parent makes it safe for the Wounded Child to share information.

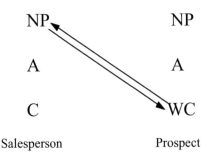

Salesperson   Prospect

Vision of Solution

In this step the salesperson, through his questions, is able to help the prospect determine his ideal situation. The salesperson is in the Nurturing Parent Ego State and the prospect is still in the Wounded Child Ego State.

Remember, the Child Ego State is the keeper of creativity. The salesperson should help the prospect determine his best creative solution to his P.A.I.N.

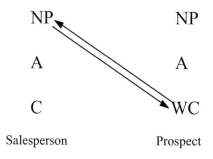

Investment

The Investment step is often difficult for the salesperson to address. The reason it can be difficult is because of our rules/scripts from the Critical Parent, such as, "It is impolite to talk about money, Money is the root of all evil, Money is a private issue, etc." Another reason it can be difficult to talk about money is that our Adapted Child starts to act up. We may, at a subconscious level, fear losing the prospect's approval.

It is crucially important for a salesperson to address the money issue before she moves any further along in the sales process. Remember, there are four necessary components for a qualified prospect. He must have P.A.I.N., you must have a solution for his P.A.I.N., he must have money, and he must be willing and able to make a decision. It is in your best interest and your prospect's best interest to have this discussion. This discussion should be done in an Adult-to-Adult transaction (note parallel transaction).

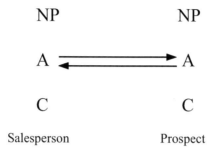

NP   NP

A   A

C   C

Salesperson   Prospect

Decision

Obviously, you must be talking to a decision maker who is willing to make a decision. The important thing to remember in this step is to stay in an Adult-to-Adult transaction. If you ask the prospect if he is the decision maker, he will most often say yes to protect his ego. This may force him to move into his Child (Rebel) Ego State, which will cause a crossed transaction. The more appropriate question to ask would be, "What is the decision process you would use to make a decision in this price range." Companies go about repeating history when it comes to decision-making. They usually follow a set procedure.

Major Contract

The Major Contract is merely a checkpoint for the salesperson to reflect upon whether he has covered all of his bases. In order to do this, the salesperson must be in his Adult Ego State. Remember, the Adult Ego State is analytical and methodically goes about answering who, what, when, where, why, and how. The Adult is also capable of determining consequences and assessing whether or not a mutually profitable outcome can be achieved. The purpose of this step in the process is to determine:

- Whether you have covered all of the necessary steps so that your prospect is qualified

- What needs to be in your Proof of Presentation to win the sale

- What happens after you do the presentation

Proof of Presentation

In this step of the process, the salesperson moves into Nurturing Parent addressing the prospect's P.A.I.N. The salesperson is also cascading between Nurturing Parent and Adult. When presenting the solution, the salesperson is in Adult. When talking about the P.A.I.N. the salesperson is in Nurturing Parent.

The prospect moves into his Wounded Child because his P.A.I.N. is brought to the forefront. He is determining whether you are able to get him out of his P.A.I.N. His Adult is also analyzing whether your solution will bring him the desired result. People make emotional decisions

for logical reasons.

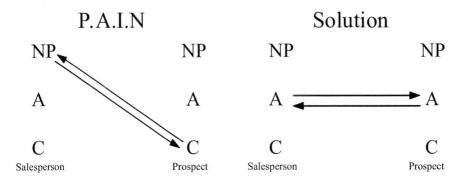

Retention

This step is designed to keep the prospect from feeling

Buyer's Remorse and to keep life-long customers. It is

important in this stage for both parties to be communicating

in an Adult-to-Adult manner. *Refer to buying phases.* The

last phase of buying is the *measurement phase.* Once a

decision to purchase has been made, the buyer immediately

begins the process of assessing whether he has made a good

decision.

When a prospect makes a decision to purchase, understand the Child Ego State buys (Buying is emotional), the Parent Ego State gives permission to buy, and the Adult Ego State analyzes data to determine intellectually whether it is a good decision.

Child: "I want it, I want it."

Parent: "You are allowed. You didn't make a hasty decision."

Adult: "It makes intellectual sense to do this. The data computes."

The Retention Phase starts immediately after the decision to buy is made and continues indefinitely.

Questioning

Much is written about the art of asking questions. Indeed, the art of asking questions the right way has been addressed in previous chapters. However, if one is to truly understand how to ask the right questions, one must understand that there are two perspectives that must be considered before one becomes adept at asking the right questions. The first is questioning from the prospect's perspective and the second is questioning from the salesperson's perspective. Let's talk about the prospect's perspective first.

The Prospect's Prospective

An iceberg is used as a metaphor to help you understand

what is occurring when a customer asks you a question. As

you look at the iceberg you will notice that the mass

beneath the water is much greater than the mass above the water. If you will recall, it was the mass of ice below the surface that was responsible for the sinking of the Titanic. When a customer asks you a question, that question (metaphorically, the tip of the iceberg) may not be the <u>real</u> question. Your job as a salesperson is to find out what the intent is behind the question (metaphorically, what lies beneath the surface of the water). If you are able to determine the prospect's intent you will gain insight to what the <u>real</u> question might be.

Let's take the example of a man coming home from work. He asks his wife the simple question, "What time is dinner?" There are several possible *intents* behind the question. Let's examine the possibilities. He could mean:

- Do I have time to rest?
- Did you cook?

- Did you make something I like for dinner?

- Are we having leftovers?

- What have you done all day?

- I had a late lunch and I'm not hungry.

- Did you work as hard as I did today?

- I'm hungry and I want to eat now.

- Let's go out for dinner.

As you can see, a question as simple as, "What time is dinner?" could have numerous meanings. You may be saying to yourself, "Why not just come out and say what you mean?" The reason for that is conditioning. We have all been conditioned to "dance around" the real question. We have learned that if we ask the real question, we might cause a breakdown in communication.

The Truth About Language

Language is a remarkable tool that helps us interact with other people. However, language can be misused, misunderstood, and non-productive because different words mean different things to different people. So it is with questions.

Often, when we ask a question of another person, there is an entire thought process that has taken place prior to asking the question. This thought process is often times at the subconscious level. For instance, let's use this question as an example: "How much is your product or service?" That seems to be a very simple straightforward question. Or, is it? Let's look at some possible interpretations.

Possible Interpretations:

Asked too early in the process, it might just be a "Put off"

Asked after a discussion of P.A.I.N., it might mean:

- "Can I afford this?"

- "How do you want to be paid?"

- "Will this fit within my budget?"

- "How do you compare to your competition?"

- "Is this product or service of value?"

- "Is this cost-justified?"

There might be other invisible issues that would cause a prospect to ask this question. What's important for the salesperson to remember is that the question is the "tip of the iceberg." It is a summary of the thinking that lies behind it. The question, then, is a form of verbal shorthand. It is a "complex equivalent", which represents a whole line of thinking.

In the above example, how the salesperson answers that question would be completely dependent upon why it was asked. While some of the reasons for the question may seem insignificant, others show a high level of importance. In every case, however, you won't know unless you dig below the surface to find the "question behind the question." So, before you answer, ask another question to find out the real question. This is called a Redirection. You will find out more about this later in the chapter.

Why Don't We Ask The Real Question?

Who among us has not been made to feel stupid by asking a question? How many times have we tried to explain our thinking about a certain question we had, only to have the other person become irritated and tell us to get to the bottom line? How many times have we been reprimanded for asking too many questions? Most of us fear looking stupid or ignorant if we ask a question. To protect ourselves, we ask superficial questions. We also fear being taken advantage of, so we mask our true intentions with these summary questions or "complex equivalents".

Not only does this theory apply to our prospects, it applies to us as well. The lessons we have received through experience have formed our attitudes about questions and will have an impact on us as we sell. Salespeople fear asking questions of the prospect for the same reasons that the prospect fears asking questions of the salesperson. When this dysfunctional attitude strikes a salesperson, he is quite capable of doing the "SPEW", but never really uncovering the issues. The consequence of this behavior is very low closing percentages, due to inappropriate

284

presentations being made to non-qualified prospects---

Working hard, not working smart.

Power Principle:
Any question a prospect asks you has significance related
to P.A.I.N.
You must dig to discover that significance.

Prospects have also learned this lesson. They don't want to

feel vulnerable "to getting in trouble" so they try to protect

themselves. Prospects protect themselves by asking non-

threatening questions to obtain information from you to

help them determine if you may be able to help them. The

prospect may even give you indications of P.A.I.N., but

will seldom share his real P.A.I.N. with you until he feels

he can trust you with the information.

Prospects learn how much you care by how much you try to

understand them, not by how hard you try to sell.

Presenting too early sends a very clear message of your desires.

Power Principle:
People don't care how much you know until they know how much you care.

Exercise:

Write the five most common questions you receive from your prospect.

1. _____

_____

2. _____

_____

3. _____

_____

4. _____

_____

5. _____

_____

List three possible intentions behind each question:

1. _____

   _____

   _____

2. _____

   _____

   _____

3. _____

   _____

   _____

Example:

    Prospect: "Do you do in-service training?"

    Possible Meaning: My people are going to be resistant.

                           Will I have to train my people?

                           I'm not sure I know how to use this.

This looks difficult.

Is there an added cost you are not telling me about?

It is important to understand that the question the prospect asks you is the "complex equivalent" of a deeper question. * Your job as a salesperson is to uncover his intent behind asking that question. In so doing, you will start to gain an understanding of what the prospect's real P.A.I.N. is and how to help him.

How is that accomplished? By asking the right questions the right way, at the right time. People will try to code their messages and responses for their own protection. So to get at the root of the real problem it usually will take a minimum of three questions. Often, a salesperson will hear a surface problem and immediately go into expounding upon a solution---THE SPEW. When this happens, the salesperson begins to act as an authority and starts doling out advice. In so doing, the salesperson inadvertently pressures the prospect to do problem solving before he is emotionally ready to do so. If this happens, the prospect may view the salesperson as pushy, conniving and manipulative. Unfortunately, the relationship is thus broken.   The prospect may start to feel trapped and be forced to move into denial or avoidance.

If the prospect moves into an avoidance or denial mode, no one's needs will be met.

*Power Principle:
The initial problem the prospect brings you is never the real problem.

The Salesperson's Perspective

Sometimes, the prospect may lack problem-solving skills or may be too emotionally tied into his problem to determine the best solution. Ideally, the salesperson should act as a facilitator in the problem solving process. To accomplish this it is imperative for the salesperson to listen intently to what the prospect is saying. As we listen, our job is really to discover how the speaker views his situation, what his feelings are, and what his thoughts are about his particular situation. Then our questions can be directed to the speaker's orientation rather than the salesperson's agenda and desire to get the business. It is important to remember that your intent to help the prospect discover an ideal solution is more important than any sales techniques you might want to use. If indeed, your focus is to help the prospect, all else will take care of itself.

Questions can be abrasive and can come off sounding like an interrogation. Discovery Selling® was designed to help you avoid sounding like an interrogator. The Ground Rules sets the stage for you to ask questions. Getting permission to ask questions is crucial and will help you create an environment that is safe. It will give you some insight into what to ask to bring the P.A.I.N. to the surface. Also, if you recall from the Relationship module, trust consists of Sincerity, Honesty, and Competence. *Refer to the Doctor Story on pg. 132 of the Ground Rules Module.* Competence is determined by your ability to ask the right questions the right way at the right time.

While asking questions, it is important to realize that you, the salesperson, should design your questions so that they progress up the pain pyramid.

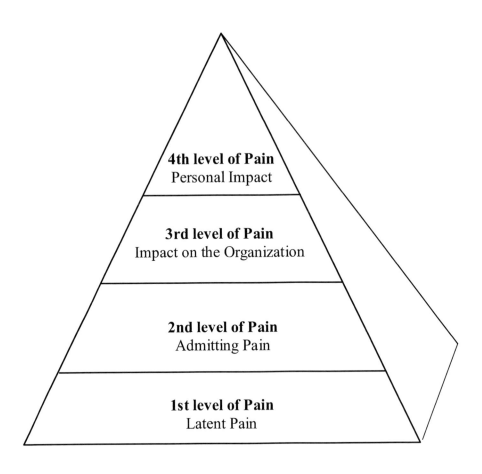

You will oftentimes start the sales interaction with the prospect in level one or level two, latent P.A.I.N. or admittance of P.A.I.N. What will distinguish you from the average salesperson will be your ability to transfer to impact questions. Once you become adept at asking impact questions at the right time, you will be able to measurably increase your closing percentage.

Neil Rackham, a social psychologist and founder of Huthwaithe Institute conducted a twelve-year $1,000,000 research project studying the most effective practices in selling. He studied 35,000 salespeople in a broad range of industries. These industries were all selling high dollar ($500 or more) items and services. His objective was to determine what separated the top 20% of performers from average performers. What he discovered was that indeed, the art of asking questions was important. However, even more important was the type of questions the salesperson asked.

He noted that the average performers asked mainly *information questions* that were intellectual in nature, for example, "What type of equipment do you use? How many employees do you have? How long have you been in business? What type of services do you provide?" He was able to determine that information questions had very little affect on the successful outcome of a sale and could actually negatively impact success. Information questions are extremely annoying to the prospect since they are educational in nature. Much of this information can be obtained through sources readily available. DO YOUR HOMEWORK before the sales call.

Rackman also determined that many salespeople asked questions that were directed at problems on a call. For example, "Is your equipment hard to use? Do you have a high turnover rate with employees? Are you satisfied with the growth of your company? What is not working? Where do you have breakdowns in your system, etc?"

Salespeople, who used these types of questions and were able to offer solutions, were slightly more successful, but mainly in smaller dollar sales. However, *problem questions* had little affect on larger dollar sales, and did not necessarily produce favorable outcomes.

As his research continued, he further concluded that salespeople who were most successful in large dollar sales were the salespeople who were adept at asking *impact questions*. Impact questions are emotionally based and able to help the prospect determine consequence to his P.A.I.N. Therefore, having the ability to help the prospect move up the pyramid and discover how a particular P.A.I.N. is impacting him would be more effective in producing a positive outcome.

There are two types of questions that can help you get to the intent of your prospects questions--closed-ended and open-ended questions. A closed- ended question will be answered with a simple response that may end the conversation. It is used to help clarify information. The second type of question is the open-ended question. This is a question that your prospect has to answer with a statement, more that just a yes or no. Open-ended questions begin with *who, what, when, where, and how.* They can also begin with "why". "Why" questions can be tricky because they might make the prospect become defensive. The prospect may feel like he needs to defend his previous actions or decisions. There are times when "why" questions can be used to clarify an answer or statement; however they can be cushioned by saying "Could you help me understand why...?

Salespeople have often been taught that the only questions they should ask are open-ended questions, not closed-ended questions. Both are appropriate however, depending upon the situation. The power of the question lies not in whether the question is open or closed, but in whether it is addressing an area that is emotionally important to the prospect and the perceived intent of the salesperson in asking it.

You now have become aware of the different kinds of questions. You have the knowledge as to what kinds of questions will bring you positive results. Now it is time to develop the skill of asking effective questions, which is much different than having the mere knowledge of what constitutes an effective question.

There is a formula that will be helpful when a prospect throws you a question or makes a statement to which you feel a need to respond. Our formula for responding is to Validate, Cushion, and Redirect. When you **validate** what someone says to you, in essence you are confirming that you understand the question or statement. Prior to responding, you must make sure you are responding to his true question or statement (intent). In addition, if your true intent is to help the prospect, you must get to the root of the question or statement. This is accomplished by redirecting your response and asking a question of the prospect. Remember, we must keep the doors of communication open, keep the prospect OK, and *nurture, nurture, nurture.* Cushion your response and then redirect your answer with a question.

For example:

<u>In response to a statement:</u>

Prospect says: *"My biggest challenge is _____."*

Salesperson cushions with: *"I can understand how that could be a challenge,"*

Then redirects with: *"Could you explain that a bit further?"*

<u>In response to a question:</u>

Prospect says: *"Will your product/service accomplish _____?*

Salesperson cushions with: *"Excellent question,"*

Then redirects with: *"You probably asked that for a reason. Could you share it with me?*

Other possible Cushioning statements:

<u>In response to statements:</u>

That makes a lot of sense.

I know exactly how you feel.

I can appreciate that.

That is an excellent point.

I appreciate your candor in sharing that with me.

Good insight.

You seem to have a really good handle on the situation.

In response to questions:

Good question, that's important.

I'm glad you asked me that.

I was hoping you were going to bring that up.

Sounds like you have really done your homework...I don't get that question very often.

The following is a conversation between a salesperson and their prospect using cushioning and redirection.

Prospect:	"What differentiates you from your competition?"
S.P.: Cushion:	"Excellent question"

Redirect:	"Who else are you currently looking at?
Prospect:	"We're looking at A, B, and C."
S.P.: Cushion: Redirect:	"Good choices," "If you were making a decision today, which I know you aren't, which would you be leaning toward?
Prospect:	"Vendor A"
S.P.: Cushion: Redirect:	"Oh! Interesting." "What makes them stand out?"
Prospect:	"We like their in-service training."
S.P.: Cushion: Redirect:	"I understand they do a fine job in that area." "Help me understand what you like about them?"
Prospect:	"We also like their low cost."
S.P.: Cushion:	"Low cost in comparison to what?"
Prospect:	"We haven't looked at anything else. Their price seemed quite reasonable."

S.P.:	"Help me understand, what does reasonable mean?"
Prospect:	Their price seems fair.
S.P. Redirect:	It might well be. "When you spoke to them about the _____ (*insert a possible problem*) their clients experienced, what did they tell you?"

At this point, the salesperson will start uncovering primary concerns. This may be an oversimplification, however, it is written to illustrate the necessity of moving toward something substantial to uncover P.A.I.N.*

*Power Principle:
Anything you need to say to a prospect can be conveyed in the form of a question.

One can decipher from the above example, that the buyer is probably in either phase two or three of the Buy Cycle—Satisfaction Criteria or Evaluate Options. The reason for taking the time to redirect the prospect's questions is to remove the barriers and uncover the prospect's real reasons for leaning toward the competitor. Cushioning will keep the prospect from feeling a need to defend his intellectual reasoning. In the above conversation, the salesperson has set the stage for further discussion. The salesperson can now discuss his competitive advantage that he has over the competition and perhaps even create a preference toward his product and company.

What does a Redirection accomplish for you?

_____

_____

What does a Redirection accomplish for the prospect?

_____

_____

Exercise:

Listed below are common questions sales representatives are frequently asked. Determine what your cushioning statement and redirect should be for each question.

1. Why should I use *your product/service* over my current company?

2. What are you going to do for me that is different?

3. Why is *your product/service* so much more expensive?

4. I don't see the dollar value in all of this.

Remember...

- Never Defend Your Position

- Tonality Is Critical

- Intent Is More Important Than Technique

- Your Responsibility Is To Help The Prospect Through The Discovery Process®

Vision Of Solution

Imagine for a moment that you are a defense attorney representing a defendant who faces a serious offense and a lengthy prison sentence if convicted. Prior to the opening of the trial, you have the opportunity to sit and visit with the jurors. During your visit, you ask them their feelings and thoughts about the case, what type of evidence they would like to see, how they would like to have the trial presented, and what they would need to see, hear and feel in order to return a not guilty verdict in favor of your client. This knowledge would give you the ability to present a very compelling case specifically tailored to this jury in this trial and probably win the case for your client.

Of course, that activity is highly illegal. Because it would give you, the defense, such a strong advantage over the prosecution, it is not permitted. Jury tampering could cost you your law license, huge fines and even jail time.

Your prospect is the jury. He is the judge as well. Fortunately in sales, the rules of law do not apply. You <u>do</u> have the opportunity to conduct such an interview, to stack the odds so strongly in favor of your solution that it will be hard for the competition to win. Unfortunately, most salespeople often neglect this vital step and an opportunity is missed.

Revisiting the Sales Definition

Selling is the art and science of inspiring the prospect to do what is in his best interest through discovering what is in his best interest on a personal and emotional level.

Before you deliver your formalized presentation, either oral or written, make sure you get together with the prospect to determine what is in their best interest. In so doing, your solution will become so compelling, that other solutions the prospect might investigate will appear to be inferior versions by comparison.

The ultimate purpose of the Vision of Solution step in the selling process is to get the prospect to help you develop a plan or proposal that he will buy.

Discovering P.A.I.N. (Satisfaction Gaps—the difference between expectation and reality) should invariably lead to a discussion of possible solutions. Too often, salespeople are entirely too eager to do a proposal, prior to uncovering P.A.I.N. When a salesperson falls into this trap he moves his product or service to the level of a commodity. Once you are at a commodity level, the only difference between you and your competitor is price. To avoid this trap, you must complete a number of additional activities to fully qualify the prospect and help him become committed to your solution.

That's the purpose for the P.A.I.N. finding step and the reason it comes before Vision of Solution. Once an individual discovers a problem or an opportunity and makes a commitment to address the gap, it is time to explore potential solutions. But, what is a solution?

While your prospect may not know the specifics of the solution, he will often have an idea of the preferred result he is attempting to achieve. By asking, "What do you see as the best possible outcome?" he will usually begin describing the kind of results he would like to achieve. In this step of the selling process, we can begin asking questions that would "test" his reaction to some of the ways we might be able to help.

Features and Benefits

It might be helpful here to briefly discuss Features and Benefits and correct some misunderstandings that may exist. Feature and benefit selling has long been held as the best possible way to sell. "Stress your features and benefits'" sales trainers would tell you. The thinking goes, "If the prospect just understood how wonderful your products are, they would insist on buying from you. So just educate them." The fatal flaw here is that the prospect understands your features and benefits. Not at an intellectual level, but at an application level. He'll probably be thinking to himself, "Gee, this is nice. If I ever need this, I guess I should call these folks." He does not

understand its application to his situation.

Power Principle:
Solutions have no intrinsic value. The value of a solution is
derived from the problem it solves or the results that it
creates. It must be objectively measurable.

Features and benefits are usually generic in nature; i.e. they

are inherent or built in to the product or service. They're

part of its design. While you can communicate them to

your prospects, they usually sound like a lot of bragging

and overselling and are seen as a great deal of hyperbole.

Features and benefits will, when used inappropriately and

at the wrong time, usually lead to a litany of objections.

Salespeople may see them as presenting solutions, but

prospects too often see them as a "hard sell" tactic.

The problem is not that features and benefits have little or no value; it's just that they don't have meaning because they exist primarily in the salesperson's mind, NOT in the prospect's mind. Unless and until the prospect takes ownership of those F & B's, they will usually be meaningless (not worthless).

Redefining Features and Benefits

A **_feature_** is something that is built in to or inherent in the product or service being offered. "Our widget is light weight." A feature is a standard that can be stated rather explicitly to almost any prospect to whom you talk

A feature has traditionally been interchanged and thought of as a benefit (the reason you should care about the feature). In reality, the "reason" is actually the advantage.

An _**advantage**_ puts some teeth in the feature, by trying to stress its importance so the prospect says, "Oh wow!"

Example:

"Our Widget is light weight, so you can easily move it around."

An advantage therefore is just like a feature. It's part of the product (not something that is customized) and hopefully adds something important to the feature. An advantage is positioned in the salesperson's mind with the assumption that the prospect cares.

A _**benefit**_ is how the F & A assist in solving the prospect's P.A.I.N.

Example:

"Our Widget is light weight, so you can easily move it around, thus eliminating the need to have three Widgets at different points in your building."

Note, the Benefit statements tie directly back to the prospect's stated P.A.I.N. Therefore, the acid test to determine if you can make a benefit statement is whether or not the prospect has a stated P.A.I.N. which the Feature and Advantage helps him address.

Remember, Features and Advantages are in the salesperson's mind. A benefit is in the prospect's mind. Benefits are the way that Features and Advantages derive value because they become a solution. Solutions are worth more than a product or a service

Exercise:

To support this notion, refer back to J.P. Guilford's three stages of decision-making and see if you can connect these concepts to that model of progression. What stage of decision- making is the Vision of Solution? Why?

_____

_____

_____

Testing For Features and Advantages

During the Proof Presentation (the next step in the sales process), it is foolish to stress features or advantages that are meaningless to the prospect. They will only gain you a string of objections, many of which cannot be answered, and usually cause the prospect to believe he could be paying too much.

Power Principle:
People always perceive a product as being too expensive if it has more features than they want.

Let's say you're looking to buy a new car, but you absolutely, positively DO NOT WANT power windows, a top of the line sound system, heated seats, or tinted windows. But, the salesperson believes these are wonderful options for you and insists on trying to convince you of their value. But you're thinking to yourself, "I'm going to be paying for things I do not want". What's worse, the more the salesperson tries to convince you of their grandeur, the less you like the person…often to the point of contempt if he goes too far.

The better way is to introduce your Features and Advantages as questions to test their importance. Let's use our previous example. "You mentioned that you'd like some mobility in your next widget so that you could move it to different departments, thus saving you money by allowing you the need to invest in only one widget. How important is the weight of that widget?"

The traditionalists have always portrayed closed-ended questions as anathema; however they are powerful when used at the right time and in this instance a yes or a no is exactly what you need. Closed-ended questions are ones that help you test for the importance of a specific Feature or Advantage. Once it is important and is related to solving a P.A.I.N., it becomes a Solution and provides a Benefit.

Once you are able to help the prospect create his Vision of Solution, you are now ready to give him/her the ideal solution that will fit his needs. You can now begin the process of preparing for your presentation. We refer to this step of the process as Proof. It is now your job to provide the proof to the prospect that you can indeed address and alleviate his P.A.I.N. However, before any solutions (proof) are presented it is necessary to have a serious money discussion, because PRICE ALWAYS COUNTS!

Investment

Up to this point in the program the authors have spent considerable time delving into the qualification process. We know that a prospect is qualified when four criteria are met. He must:

1. Have and admit P.A.I.N.;

2. Be willing to decide to do something about the P.A.I.N.;

3. You and your company must have a solution for the P.A.I.N.;

4. He must have money and be willing to make the necessary investment to alleviate his P.A.I.N.

This chapter is all about the investment that is required by the prospect and the salesperson in order to consummate a sale. Investment doesn't mean just money; it means time, energy, and resources. Time and energy are very real commodities that must be guarded and used wisely. The salesperson will be able to decide if the prospect is worth spending more time and energy with him if the prospect admits P.A.I.N. Once P.A.I.N. has been admitted, the prospect must come to realize and admit the impact of the P.A.I.N. If the impact is great enough to warrant further discussions, the salesperson knows that he must continue to invest his time and energy to help the prospect create his ideal vision of how he would like his problem solved. When the salesperson has progressed to this stage, it is imperative that he has a money discussion with the prospect.

Too often salespeople either talk money too soon in the process or wait too late in the sales process before addressing it. There are only two times when the investment should be discussed--**after P.A.I.N and then again during Proof of Presentation step.**

Money Mistakes

A prospect may ask the salesperson right up front how much his product or service costs. Often times, the salesperson will answer the prospect prior to determining exactly what the prospect needs. If the salesperson succumbs to the prospect's demands, the prospect will usually look at your price as too expensive. In his mind, your product may be no different than your competitors. They may be looking at your product or service as nothing more than an article of trade, which by the way, is the way Webster's defines *commodity*. If you answer the prospect prior to getting P.A.I.N. on the table, you have just allowed the prospect to put your product at the commodity level.

Power Principle:
Giving price too early will only hurt you.

The Commodity Slide-The Product Life Cycle

Use history as a lesson. At the turn of the 20th century, our economy was moving from an agrarian society to an industrial society. Farmers were forced to leave their farms and go work in factories. The farmers had to find an expedient way to get to work. They tried using their mules for transportation; however, the mules too often did not cooperate.

Solution Phase

Along came Henry Ford who recognized the problem and created a solution to the societal problem. If the pain of getting to the factory was great enough, people would find a way to purchase a car, which would be an ideal solution. We could say that **once the problem was recognized along with its impact,** Henry Ford **provided a solution**.

All of his cars were the same price and the same color. He was known for his saying, "You could buy my car in any color as long as it is black." The question the customer asks when a product is in the solution phase is, "How can I get one?"

Differentiation Phase

After some time passed, some engineer-minded people purchased one of Henry's cars. The "engineers" took Ford's car apart, put it back together and realized that they too could make a car and in turn, sell it. Only, they also realized that they **could make it a little different**, perhaps change the color. In so doing they would be able to achieve a competitive advantage. The question the customer asks when a product is in the differentiation phase is, "Which one do I want based on the choices that are available?"

Commodity Phase

Fast-forward in history to the year 2002. We now have the capabilities to look on the Internet to find the exact car we want at the **cheapest price**. Therefore, one might say that cars are currently at the commodity level (an article of trade). The only difference, once we know our satisfaction criteria, is **price.** The question the customer asks when a product is in the commodity phase is, "How much is it?"

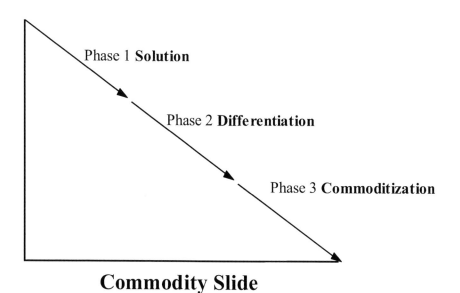

Commodity Slide

When we talk about price too early in the sales cycle, we are inadvertently moving our product to the level of a commodity (an article of trade) in the consumer's mind. The customer has learned it is in her best interest to position your product as a commodity. Once at the commodity level, the only difference between you and your competitor is price and therefore, even if she wants your product, she is positioned to buy it at a lower price. No doubt your company has invested significant resources to provide a premium product or service that stresses quality and value. If you have a quality product or service, it will cost more. If the prospect thinks you are just like your competitor (commodity) there would be no reason for her to use your product or service.

You must stay at the top of the commodity slide and position yourself to bring *solutions* to your clients. Remember *solutions* without P.A.I.N. have no value. Use history as your teacher. Henry Ford brought *solutions* to the consumer after there was a recognized P.A.I.N. So before you talk price, have a serious discussion about P.A.I.N. It worked for Henry and countless others, it will work for you.

Power Principle:
Solutions have no inherent value. They derive value from the problems they solve or the results they achieve.

As salespeople we have to understand that **price is always important**. However statistically, when buyers are asked where price ranked in their decision process, they answered fourth or fifth. So, what we do know is price is not the most important, but it is important.

Common Sales Mistakes

Example:

Let's move out of your world for a moment and move into the real estate world. Assume you have decided you can afford a $150,000 house, even though you have qualified for up to a $175,000 loan. You feel that if you went that high the payments would put a strain on you financially. So you have decided to look at homes between a $150,000-$155,000. You and your spouse go to a realtor; the realtor shows you a $400,000 home. Do you have a fit? No. Does price count? You bet. Would you want to continue working with this agent? Probably not, she has blown it.

You go to another realtor and she takes you to see three homes priced at $145,000, $152,000, and $157,000. You like the $157,000 home the best. Is it in your range? Probably. You start justifying why the $157,000 home would be better for you. You find a way to make it happen. SOLD!

This example may sound somewhat ridiculous at first; however, how many times do we as salespeople act similar to the first scenario in the above example? Are we as salespeople ever guilty of presenting a solution that is totally out of the prospects range?

Another mistake salespeople make is they don't talk about money before they do a presentation. This moves them into the "Hope and Pray" arena. They hope the price won't be a problem to the prospect; and they pray it will be close to what the prospect was anticipating and within their budget range. They are also hoping that there won't be too great of a discrepancy between their price and the competition's price.

To avoid the common money mistakes, you must have the money discussion prior to your presentation, proposal or demo. The first time you discuss money is after you have been able to uncover P.A.I.N. and have helped the prospect create his Vision of Solution. Remember you are going through the qualification process. Money is obviously part of the process. In the P.A.I.N. / G.A.I.N. section you learned that it is imperative for you to discover what the prospect's P.A.I.N. is costing him. You don't want to offer a solution that is much more expensive than the cost of the P.A. I. N. or not appropriate for the buyer's budget (remember the real estate example).

Power Principle:
Price always counts.

The Price Objection

Throughout our years of training thousands of salespeople, the number one challenge that we hear is that of overcoming the price objection. The price objection usually surfaces after the salesperson has invested an inordinate amount of time, energy and resources into the project. Too often the price objection happens because the salesperson has not used the sales process and has presented before having a serious money discussion. When price becomes the issue, the typical reaction of the salesperson is either drop the price or start espousing the features and advantages of the product.

In the case of the former, the salesperson drops the price, the unspoken message is that the price was unfairly inflated and the salesperson was trying to gouge the prospect. The trust relationship is now on the decline. If the salesperson happens to get the business, he has just set a precedent for future sales with the client.

If the salesperson chooses the latter response and starts defending his price, he will typically start espousing features and advantages of his product or service. Features and advantages position the salesperson in a mode of defense. If you will recall, an OK/Not OK principle is NEVER DEFEND. When you defend you force the prospect into a mode of having to defend his position. In any event, it becomes confrontational.

Exercise:

Reflect on what makes the money discussion difficult. List the barriers you find in discussing money:

_____

_____

_____

_____

Are these actual barriers or are they conceptual barriers? Only you can determine the answer.

Some Additional Money Barriers

Salespeople:

- Don't understand how to compare the price of their product against the value of the solution to the prospect (Products are comparatively shopped for price, solutions are impossible to compare).

- Sell products, not solutions

- Think what they sell costs a lot so they overreact to a price flinch*

- Make too many assumptions about the investment step

- Are not prepared to reassure the buyer the price is fair, reasonable, and non-negotiable

- Are uncomfortable talking about money

- Have personal doubts about the value of the product

- See the value of their product and assume the prospect will as well

- Fear the prospect

- Believe the flinch*

- Take the path of least resistance

*Flinch: an overreaction by the prospect when you present your price. Its primary purpose is to scare the salesperson into lowering his price.

Salespeople, as a general rule, are overly sensitive to price. When the prospect flinches, they will often give a discount. Discounting causes problems for several reasons.

1. The trust factor comes into play. By discounting, you inadvertently start breaking down trust. The message to the prospect is that you originally overpriced your product at their expense.

2. Discounting also sets a precedent for future sales.

3. The salesperson believes discounting will get the sale but it often doesn't. If the salesperson doesn't get something in return for discounting his product, he may cause the prospect to lose respect for him and ultimately damage the relationship. No one wants to do business with a needy salesperson.

4. Many sales reps take the path of least resistance by giving a quick price concession, believing that if they do discount, it will be a favor that the customer rewards. The customer seldom remembers the favor.

Basic Principles About Money:

- The best always cost more and everyone knows it

- When you lower the price you create cognitive dissonance. Cognitive dissonance is confusion. The customer is thinking, "Is it a better product or a cheaper product?" It is impossible to have it both ways, and they know it. When you lower price you reduce the quality of your product.

- When you lower the price, it sends signals to the buyer that you are not a believer in the value of what you sell

- It takes no talent to lower price

- If you are not getting some price objections, you are going in too cheap. Raise your prices!

- If you get the business on price, you will lose the business on price

- Once you have discounted, you will always have to discount

- If price is your selling advantage, you will never have a long-term competitive advantage

Getting Money on the Table

Many times salespeople have a hard time bringing up money. So many of us have been scripted to not talk about money. Our parents may have told us it is impolite to ask anyone questions about how much they earn or how much they have spent on certain items. There are verses in the Bible that talk about the evils associated with money. It is no wonder money is a difficult subject to bring up. However, if you don't bring it up after Vision of Solution it will come back to haunt you. And haunt you it will with a vengeance.

How do you introduce the topic of Investment? There are several possible entrance lines.

Author's note:

> *"When I first started in sales, it was sometimes difficult for me to bring up money. I remember my sales coach told me, 'If you feel it say it.' So, after completing the Vision of Solution step, I would say to the prospect, the following words, 'It is always difficult for me to talk about money, but you are probably wondering how much this is going to cost. When would you like to discuss it?' The prospect always said, 'This is as good a time as any.' It worked every time. "*

If you analyze the above conversation, it is a form of the Sales Rescue. A next probable question to the above statements would be, "Have you established a budget to address this project?" Their response would fall under one of three categories. They would say:

> "Yes, we have, but we don't share that information with anyone."

> "No, we don't."

> "Yes, we do, and it is _____."

Response 1

"I understand and that is certainly your right. I know every client is unique, however other clients trying to accomplish some of the same results you are tend to invest somewhere between _____ and _____. Can you see yourself falling somewhere in that range?'

Response 2

"Wow, this is going to be hard. How did you plan on paying for this?" or "Where are you going to get the money?" "How important is (revisit

P.A.I.N.)_____? I understand every organization is unique, however other clients who are trying to accomplish the same results you are, tend to invest somewhere between _____ and _____. Can you see yourself falling somewhere within that range?"

Response 3

When they share a number that is extremely low, you sigh and say: "How did you come up with that number? It is going to be difficult to deal with the issues we've discussed with that budget. Clients trying to achieve the results that we've discussed are typically prepared to invest somewhere between _____ and _____. Can you see yourself falling somewhere within that range?"

Their response will give you an indication whether to invest any more time, energy, or resources. A note of caution: Before you throw in the towel, revisit P.A.I.N. and Vision of Solution. Perhaps you can adjust their vision or deliver the solution in phases.

If they respond with a number that seems feasible, you still sigh. You don't want them to think they came in too high. You then respond with: "It is going to be a challenge, but we will most likely be able to build the solution around that budget."

If you have done a good job in communicating to the prospect that you have an honorable intent, prospects will most generally be open and friendly until you reach the Investment phase in the selling process. It is at this juncture that the prospect may start showing resistance. That is when the negotiation begins. Let's look at why salespeople get resistance at this juncture.

1. Salespeople have trained prospects that they will drop the price if the prospect flinches. Because of this, the prospect does his due diligence and objects to see if he is getting the best price available for his ideal solution.

2. Prospects don't feel the price is worth it. It is a **conviction issue** about the value of the product. If they truly believe it is worth it, they will pay you your price. An example of this is the $6000 shower curtain purchased by a CEO of a now defunct company. He obviously had the conviction that the shower curtain was worth the money. (Don't tell us people want the lowest price).

3. The buyer has doubts about the value, worth or usefulness of the solution. They don't have the conviction that the problem is great enough to warrant the costs (price, time, effort, hassle) of the solution.

4. The buyer believes he can get the same value from someone else for less.

What we often find is that when salespeople get objections on price they are not sure exactly what the reason is behind the objection. They don't know how to respond, because they don't know what motivated the buyer to make the price objection. Salespeople assume the motivation behind the objection is simply to get a lower price. That would certainly make the buyer happy, however that won't always accomplish a closed sale. A salesperson would be better off serving the needs of the client and his own needs by finding out the client's intent behind the objection. The adept salesperson addresses the real issue behind the objection. In doing so, he will have a greater chance of closing the sale without reducing his profit while simultaneously serving his client's needs.

As salespeople, it is our job to truly uncover the reason that is keeping the buyer from moving forward. How is this best done? Consider using the following question, "Usually when we get to this point in the process and we seem to be far apart on price, I find that we are really talking about a conviction issue and it usually falls into one of three categories. You don't have the conviction that:

1. My solution can really address your challenges

2. You don't believe in the value of my product

3. You feel you can get the same value somewhere else for less money.

4. Of those three, which is it?"

What you are accomplishing by statements like this is further discussion. The prospect will usually pick one of the above choices.

If the buyer picks number 1, your response needs to follow the sequence given in the chapter on Questioning. You validate, cushion, and redirect. That sounds something like: "I am really glad you're sharing your concerns with me. It is certainly an important issue. Help me understand which challenges you feel are not being addressed."

If the buyer picks number 2, your response needs to follow the sequence given in the chapter on Questioning. You validate, cushion, and redirect. "You are certainly prudent in questioning your return on investment. If I didn't have the confidence that I was getting my return, I wouldn't move forward either. Let's revisit how we arrived at those numbers and determine if you can achieve a level of comfort. If not, then perhaps we need to rethink our solution and determine if we need to modify it. Where would you like to start?"

If the buyer picks number 3, your response needs to follow the sequence given in the chapter on Questioning. You validate, cushion, redirect. "If you can get the same results somewhere else for less money it would be unwise for you to go with us. I would be thinking the same way. I guess the only way you might get hurt is if you weren't comparing apples to apples. How are you going to come to that determination?" Wait for a response. When he responds, you then say something along the line of, "If you are serious about making a decision, perhaps it would be helpful if I sit with you and help you compare. I would be willing to invest twenty minutes of my time. If at the end of that meeting, we can't find any difference, then you would be financially irresponsible to go with me. I would certainly understand your choice." This would at least give you the opportunity to bring discrepancies to your client's attention. If you have done a good job in building a trust relationship, chances are the prospect would welcome the opportunity to evaluate their risk. They will evaluate their risk with you or without you. Your chances of getting the sale are greater if the prospect is verbalizing his concern. Remember, it is a conviction issue, not a price issue.

Power Principle:
Most customers develop loyalty to a vendor because of their value proposition, but seldom because of price.

You now have had a solid discussion about money. You know whether to move forward in the selling process. You have achieved a series of mutual commitments. There is only one step left in the sales process prior to delivering your Proof Presentation - The Decision Process. There should be no surprises in the presentation or in your trial, price being one of them.

Decision- Decision Process

In the end, it all comes down to someone making a yes or no decision. You can do everything right up to this point, but if a no decision gets made, absolutely nothing changes.

It's sad to see how many sales cycles end in "no decision." What makes it particularly unfortunate is that the salesperson never fully understands why he lost the business, so instead he must guess. When salespeople are asked why they lost the business, the reason most often cited is related to the price. In reality, they got out-sold by someone who probably did a more thorough job of meeting with real decision makers.

Power Principle:
You can't sell to someone who can't buy.

The real reasons salespeople lose the business:

- Did not qualify the buyer

- Ignored the signals that the buyer favored a competitor

- Presented product, not specific solutions to admitted P.A.I.N.s

- Called on a non-decision maker

- Failed to differentiate from competition

- Never found admitted P.A.I.N.

- Failed to discuss and resolve a Primary Concern on the part of the buyer

- Ignored or never contacted key influencers in the buying organization

The Discovery Selling® process insures that you will have all of your bases covered prior to the delivery of a proposal, presentation, or demo. If you ignore the process steps, you reduce your chances of doing business, and increase the likelihood of ending up with "NO DECISION."

Qualification

There are four components necessary for a qualified prospect. They are:

- Admitted P.A.I.N. coupled with a commitment to solve

- The desired solution is one you can deliver

- Prospect has the resources (money) needed to invest in the solution

- You are speaking to a decision maker who can say no, or yes.

When we move into the Decision Process Phase of the sales process there is certain information we are seeking before our proposal, presentation, or trial.

That information is:

- Who has the power to make the final yes or no decision

- The time-frame of the decision

- Who are all decision makers involved (usually there are many)

- What criteria will this person use to decide

- What role in the decision process does each person play

- What is this organization's decision process

- What are the personal decision making styles of all the players

We will cover each of these in this module.

Decision Power

In the world of business-to-business selling, most sales are

complex, meaning that there are multiple decision makers.

While we may be lead to believe that it is a committee

decision, or everyone will decide, there is usually one

person who has the ability to cast the deciding vote. Indeed, it is not unusual for one person to have the power to overrule a committee decision. How often have you been told yes only to find out that that decision was overwritten by a person of higher power?

A power person not only has final decision power, she also has the ability to gain access to additional funding if necessary. How many times have you heard, "That's more than we have in the budget?" A power person can access money from other departments and from different places within the organization. People lower in the organization, departmental people, are stuck with their budget and usually can't do much about it except budget more for the future, get you to lower your price, or find a cheaper alternative. None of these solutions is in the buyer's best interest or yours.

It is important to find the Power Person as early in the selling process as possible. Why? Because if your competition finds him and you don't, you lose even though you have a better solution.

Decision Time Frame

Asking a simple question regarding the desired date for making a decision is so obvious and necessary in selling, one wonders why it is so seldom done. Two major reasons seem to be the cause of this happening.

- The salesperson gets excited at the opportunity and makes incorrect assumptions.

- The salesperson is afraid to ask the question for fear of hearing that he is not working on a ***real*** opportunity

When we understand decision-time frame, we can allocate our time and resources appropriately. We can also determine the true legitimacy of the opportunity. Many prospects initiate a buy-cycle months, if not years, in advance of planned implementation.

Sometimes "shopping" is a means of establishing a budget for an upcoming fiscal year (some organizations do five-year plans). Other times, it's nothing more that a "market check" to keep their current provider on their toes. At still other times, there is a pressing need to address an issue as quickly as possible (active P.A.I.N.). In other cases, it is just idle curiosity on the part of a "line-level" employee who cannot buy and cannot get anyone else interested in buying. In any of these, and other situations, not knowing the real information about decision-making can be a very costly blunder on the part of the salesperson.

Exercise:

You are speaking to a prospect, and it is currently September 16th. Let's imagine that the following dialogue has occurred between the two of you.

Salesperson: "Ideally, when would you like to have a solution totally up and functioning?" (Wait for an answer)

Prospect: "We're looking to have it working by December 1."

Salesperson: "To achieve that target, when do you think you might have to have made your final decision?

Prospect: "We'd like to have the final decision made by the middle of October. Friday the 15th is our date."

Based upon this prospect's answer what would you do?

_____

_____

_____

In this scenario it's obvious there is P.A.I.N. If you don't know what it is, because they called you, you can now ask a follow up question such as, "Seems like you're trying to get this done as soon as possible. Is there a reason for the urgency?" Listen closely, and you'll probably at least hear some surface level problems. Probe further for P.A.I.N.

Now let's imagine a reverse scenario. In response to the same time frame question as in the previous example, your prospect says the following:

Prospect: "We're looking at December of next year?"

Salesperson: "That's pretty far out. How can I help you?"

Prospect: "We're trying to establish a budget."

Based upon this prospect's answer, what would you do?

_____

_____

_____

The best course of action in this situation is to get to the reasons for the long time frame. Then set a course of action that allows you to build a relationship, speak with all of the decision-makers, and schedule the main selling activities closer to the actual date. You might also ask a question similar to this: "If by some strange coincidence, you saw, heard or experienced compelling reasons to implement a solution sooner than your desired date, would you be in a position to move that date forward?" This question might give you insight into whom the real decision maker is, if it is not the person with which you are speaking.

Another *bonus question* you can ask is, "Who initiated this process?" The initiator is probably a rung or two up the organizational ladder. It could even be the Power Person. To determine her role ask, "So what role will she play in choosing which system to implement?" The next question you can, and should ask is, "When do you think I could speak to her?" DO NOT ASK FOR PERMISSION, ASK WHEN!

If there's a high level of urgency – such as in the first scenario, there is obviously P.A.I.N. However, if there's a low level of urgency, as in the second example, based upon a decision date that goes far into the future, defer your heavy selling activities until you get closer to the actual decision date. The closer you get to the decision date, the more attentive they will be during their interactions with you.

Why defer major selling activities closer to the decision date? Because, buying is emotional. It is difficult to sustain emotions for long periods of time, certainly long enough to get the business. If your prospect gets excited about what you offer too early, he won't stay that way. You'll then have to do something to re-excite him, and that's a tough proposition if you have already dazzled him with your brilliance. (This is why presentations, proposals or demos done too far in advance lose their luster). Prospects have short memories and the intensity of P.A.I.N. dissipates. Save your best for last.

Power Principle:
Time kills deals.

If we don't understand this important decision time frame concept, it can lead to many inappropriate actions on the part of the salesperson. Among them:

- Constantly calling (harassing) a prospect and pushing for a decision long before they are prepared to give you one is an irritant that can damage a relationship. It will cause the prospect to avoid you. That may, in turn, cause you to push harder. It's a vicious spiral downward.

- Investing far too much time on a low urgency prospect. They're less interested in details the farther out they are from their decision date, so you may overload them with information too soon.

- If they have an abundance of information, you may facilitate a shopping expedition that gives them the opportunity to converse with your competitors. An educated prospect is not necessarily a better prospect.

Final Authority

It is essential to determine who has final yes-no decision-making authority. That role is significantly different from just being a decision-maker. Traditionally, salespeople ask a question such as "Will you be the decision maker?"

That's a bad question. There are three problems with asking this question.

1. It suggests to the person to whom you are speaking that they have no authority.

2. It challenges the person's ego.

3. The person will usually answer, "Yes, I am" even though they are not.

Unfortunately the question asked this way would result in you getting false information almost every time. The reason is that the prospect doesn't understand what you mean by a "decision" so they usually answer yes. This person, playing the role of initiator, may have the authority to say no, which is a decision, but may not have the authority to say, "Yes we will buy." So, as you can see, you get an answer, but it is only a half-truth.

It's important here, to understand people's positions within the Decision-Making process. The Authority/Influence

Matrix will give you a quick snapshot of the 4 different

configurations.

II A NI	**III** NA I
I NA NI	**IV** A I

In the above illustration you will see four quadrants, each

representing levels of Authority and Influence. By

authority we mean they have the ability to make a yes or no

decision. They have the spending authority. Often these

people can be identified by title. However spending may

be restricted to certain dollar amounts. When a person hits

his "spending ceiling" the authority usually goes to the next

highest level and continues upward in the organization to

the person who has spending authority for the specified amount.

By *influence* we mean that the person has the ability to influence others. They have a level of respect and credibility that can have impact on others!
They have a level of respect and credibility that can influence the opinion of others.

Quadrant I

No Authority/No Influence - Typically describes the role of a gatekeeper. These gatherers collect data typically because they have been assigned that task by a superior. These folks, however, are usually not in a position to make any type of a decision other than "no". Quadrant I prospects may not be able to help you directly but they can certainly hurt you by restricting important information, as well as others playing a more significant decision-making role. A receptionist or a secretary might fit this description.

Quadrant II

Authority/No Influence - Describes individuals that have authority but low levels of influence on others. Often they can say yes based upon their title or position but cannot, for a variety of reasons, influence the opinion and attitudes of others. A Purchasing Manager (or a comparable title or position within your industry) might fit this description.

Quadrant III

No Authority/Influence - Represents individuals who have no authority but high levels of influence. Their ideas and opinions are respected and valued and they can influence the opinions of others. They have no final decision-making authority. An example of this might be an outside consultant.

Quadrant IV

Authority/Influence - Describes individuals who have the final yes or no authority as well as the ability to sway the opinions of others. These are people who must be reached during the sales cycle, not at the expense of others, but as an important part of the selling process. While they are the best people to be involved with as early as possible, they may be the most difficult to reach since they are often insulated by those in lower level quadrants. These folks usually have an executive level title. An example might be the CFO or President.

It's common to disregard a lower level prospect perhaps in a Quadrant I capacity, but that can be a big mistake since that person may be your key to obtaining access to others with whom you need to meet. In addition, that person may be able to provide you with necessary and important information which will in turn help you provide solutions directed at specific P.A.I.N.S.

It's OK to ask a person several non-threatening questions to find her level of authority and influence. A question such as, "Who besides yourself will be involved in the final decision?" An even better question might be "Let's assume that we're successful in proving to you that we have the best possible solution and you decide you want to work with us. At that point, what would happen?" If that person cannot say "Yes" you'll normally hear who has to sign-off for the go ahead. You can then ask the person you are speaking with how best to go about arranging an introduction to that person.

When prospects understand that it is in their best interest to allow you to see the power person, they'll help you gain access. What often happens, however, is that gatekeepers see the salesperson as a threat. If that's the case, they will act as a barrier to the person with whom you must speak. You must be certain that the gatekeeper knows your intent. Your true intent is to help deliver the most appropriate solution that addresses the particular stated problem.

If the gatekeeper still denies you access, your next best strategy should be to bring the interaction to a point where she tells you, "No." Once you have been told "no" by a gatekeeper, she can no longer threaten to block you access to the power person. Often, you will discover that the power person was the person who began the investigation in the first place.

A story from one of the authors serves to illustrate this "get a no" strategy.

> *"I recall making a sales call on a bank and being invited in by a gatekeeper. The person I was speaking with had been delegated the responsibility of gathering information from several providers of training services. She was not the power person, nor the final authority and she made that very clear. It became very clear as I sought to discover the prospect's P.A.I.N. that she was severely uninformed about the specific issues that her superior was attempting to address with a training program. When I asked her who might have the answers to those queries, she said it was her boss. I asked her when she could arrange a conversation with him for me, and she stated in no uncertain terms, that would not be allowed. She had been delegated the responsibility for gathering this information and that she would do. In her mind, though he never said it to her, her boss did not want to meet with potential providers. She felt she would be derelict in her duties if she allowed "salespeople" to speak with him and that it would reflect negatively on her job performance.*
>
> *After several more failed attempts to get information, and gain access to the power person, I gracefully bowed out. I told her that I respected her decision to not let me speak to her superior. I told her that I did not agree with her decision, but I respected it. I then*

asked her to please respect my decision not to propose. I told her the issues to which she had alluded were far too important for me and my staff to guess at the appropriate solution, that for us to make any kind of an intelligent proposal, we had to have more information. We thanked each other and ended the meeting with a "no". But, that's not the end of the story.

Once she had told me "no", she could no longer threaten me and I promptly began my efforts to schedule a meeting with her superior. Surprisingly, when I finally spoke with him, he was quite eager to set an appointment. We met, I got a thorough understanding of his P.A.I.N., and as it turned out, the issues he was attempting to address were not ones with which we could help. His decision criteria would have never led him to choose my firm. It would have been a disaster for us to even try to solve his problems. I was, however, able to direct him toward several of my colleagues whose expertise aligned perfectly with his needs. I was able to convey to him our specific competencies, and I have no doubt that if he ever finds himself in a situation needing help in those areas where we can help, he will call. Another footnote to this story is that I was able to compliment his assistant on her thoroughness in finding solutions. I helped her look good and she no longer diverts my phone calls to voice mail. She turned into an ally."

Decision Making Roles – The Complex Sale

A complex sale is one where there are a number of decision makers. This adds complexity to the salesperson's job, since contact must be made with all of the people involved in the process. Understanding the roles individuals play during the decision process is important in order to discover how they impact the final yes or no decision.

Gatekeepers are the people who usually make the initial contact or inquiry with the potential suppliers. Gatekeepers can be the key to gaining information and access to people within their company who are involved in the decision process. Typically, a gatekeeper will not be the final decision maker. They do, however, act as if they have that authority. If you present only to gatekeepers, you are not really selling because you're not talking to a buyer. Gatekeepers can usually only say "no".

Technical influencers evaluate your offerings based upon technical criteria. They want to know if what you are offering meets their specs. They often are the developers of those specifications. They sometimes play the dual role of gatekeeper and technical influencer. They can be described as the "screeners".

Users are those in the organization who will actually be using the chosen solution. Users usually never have final "yes" decision-making power, but they do exert a great deal of influence over others who do have that power. Never ignore the users because if you do, and your competition doesn't, you could very well lose and not even know why. It's not unusual for there to be a number of users involved, for instance during a trial. Their satisfaction can make or break a deal.

Financial influencers have the authority and the ability to release the funds for the go ahead. Financial influencers, by title, usually occupy a higher level within the organization. They may or may not be directly involved in the process. They do however have their own criteria that must be met. Not knowing their criteria could cause you to lose the sale. There is usually only one financial influencer.

Your Champion is a person who is your torchbearer and helps you win the sale. This person is your ally, as much as you are his, and wants you to win. If you win, then he wins also, in a very subjective way. Your champion becomes your key to gaining access to people and information, and also helps influence others to your offering. A Quadrant IV person (power and authority) is your best possible choice to act as your champion. You need a champion because the more complicated the sales process becomes; the more important it is for you to receive critical information. This information may only be attainable through your champion. It is important for you to know how your champion personally benefits. Knowing this will give you an indication of how committed he is to seeing you win.

Organizational Decision Process

Organizations establish processes to achieve business results and achieve goals. Specific organizations have specific ways of making decisions. If you can get them to explain to you how they have made similar decisions in the past, then there is a great likelihood that history will repeat itself. Therefore, the question you should ask is, "Can you describe for me the process that _(name of organization)_ typically goes through when making this type of a decision?"

When asked, the person will either outline the process, or will not know. More often they will not know. That's your chance to suggest a process, based upon your experience in similar situations. You might say something like, "That's not unusual. Usually, in my experience, when a business is getting ready to implement our solution, they go through a sequence of about four steps. Let me outline them to see if they might make sense for you. First, we typically meet with all of the folks involved directly. The reason we do this is to get each person's perspective of the issues we are attempting to address. Does that sound reasonable? Next, we should make certain that our technical specifications fit your requirements. We will need to talk to your technical people. Does that sound like a logical next step?" Notice that we are suggesting the involvement of all of the influencers of this sale. Make sure that all of the bases are covered. Keep outlining until you've gotten through all of them. Then ask, "What other steps might you add to this that would be appropriate for your decision process?" Go through this step slowly and above all, make certain your prospect is comfortable. It needs to be her plan, not yours. The prospect who makes no suggestions is not taking ownership of the plan. That should be a caution to you. You've missed something. Go back to P.A.I.N., and see if you can discover what you left out.

Personal Decision Style

While organizations have specific processes for making decisions, so do individuals. These decision-making preferences are, to a large degree, determined by behavioral style. We discussed these styles in the OK-Not-OK module of Discovery Selling®. It might be worthwhile for you to review that section briefly, to refresh your memory, before proceeding.

Style Identification Tips

Dominant: assertive, impatient, big picture, looking for results, time/task oriented, extroverted

Influencer: friendly, talkative, big picture, sociable, animated, people/relationship oriented, extroverted

Steady Relator: calm, reserved, good listener, likes detail, low risk, people/relationship oriented, introverted

Conscientious: hard to read, analytical, detail oriented, focuses on information and facts, quiet and reserved, time/task oriented, introverted

The following chart will give you the information you need, by behavioral style, to elicit a decision from a particular person in a manner that is comfortable to that person. Notice the Dominant and the Conscientious view their environment as antagonistic. The Influencer and the Steady Relator view their environment as favorable. The Dominant and the Influencer are extroverted, while the Conscientious and Steady Relator are introverted.

Antagonistic

Introverted (left axis) — **Extroverted** (right axis)

C

Extroverted/Introverted: Introverted
People or Task Oriented: Task
More Direct or Indirect: Direct
Over-extensions: Critical
Geared to/Looking for:
Procedures/
Information
High C emotion: Fear
Low C emotion: No fear

D

Extroverted/Introverted: Extroverted
People or Task Oriented: Task
More Direct or Indirect: Direct
Over-extensions: Impatient
Geared to/Looking for: Results/
Efficiency
High D emotion: Anger/Short fuse
Low D emotion: Slow to anger/
Long fuse

S

Extroverted/Introverted: Introverted
People or Task Oriented: People
More Direct or Indirect: Indirect
Over-extensions: Possessiveness
Geared to/Looking for: Trust/
relationship
High S emotion: Non-emotional
Low S emotion: Emotion

I

Extroverted/Introverted: Extroverted
People or Task Oriented: People
More Direct or Indirect: Indirect
Over-extensions: Disorganization
Geared to/Looking for: Fun,
the experience
High I emotion: Optimism
Low I emotion: Pessimism
High I value: Trust
Low I value: Distrust

Favorable

Using the following graph, first observe the person's behavior. Once you have done this, you will be able to refer to the Decision Style table on the following graph for specific ideas on how to influence this person, how to structure your meetings and conversations, and most of all, how to build a mutually productive relationship.

Decision Styles by Behavioral Style

	Dominant	Influencer	Steady Relator	Cautious Thinker
Change	Creates it	Likes It	Dislikes It	Accepts It With Great Hesitation
Products	Gets Results/ Increase Profits/ Creates Control	Newest/ Biggest/ Flashiest/ Highest Quality	Helps the Team/ No Frills	Gadgets/ Quantitative/ Well Engineered
Meeting Style	Quick/ To The Point	Friendly/ Informal	Reserved Yet Friendly	Controlled/ Stoic
Group Discussion	Tries to Control	Tries to Influence	Tries to Appease	Tries to Inform
Work Habits	Creates the Flow	Goes with the Flow	Routine	Rigid
Level of Assertiveness	Aggressive	Assertive	Passive	Quietly Assertive on Points
Negotiation Focus	Results/ Control	Involvement/ Popular	Stability/ Peace	Analysis/ Be Right
Buying Direction (motivation)	Normally Moving Towards	Normally Moving Towards	Normally Moving Away	Normally Moving Away

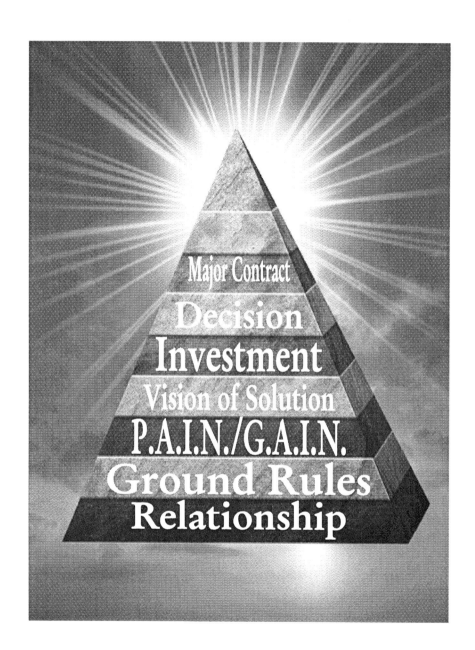

Major Contract

You have probably gotten the message by now---Qualify, Qualify, Qualify. Qualification is a process, not an event, that is continual and incremental. At this point you may be saying to yourself that just about every chapter in the book opens with the necessity of qualifying. You might even be saying that the authors are being somewhat redundant. Well, if you are, then you have been a good student because every time you progress up the pyramid, you are moving one step closer to a closed sale. We all know that closing sales is the only way any of us make money.

Throughout all our years of training salespeople, we invariably hear that they want to learn how to close more effectively. Closing always surfaces as one of the biggest challenges faced by salespeople. It is a challenge because too often salespeople have over-invested time, energy and resources without getting any commitments from the prospect. Discovery Selling® has been designed to help you obtain a series of commitments so that when it is time to close, closing is just another mini-commitment.

The commitments you have received up to this point should just about seal the sale provided you are able to provide a solution to the prospect's P.A.I.N. (Note, you have not done a presentation, proposal, or a demo/trial yet). How do you as a salesperson know you are ready to show your brilliance in providing the perfect solution? You know by taking the time to debrief yourself to determine if indeed you have covered all of your bases. This step is so important that it was built into the sales process. **The Major Contract is the contract you make with yourself to slow down and determine if, indeed, you have a qualified prospect and** have achieved the necessary agreements to move forward into your **Proof Presentation.**

The **Major Contract** enables the salesperson to determine if the four necessary qualification components (P.A.I.N., Money, Decision, and Solution for a Prospect) have been met and to determine if the prospect is ready for a presentation or trial.

Debrief Checklist for Qualification

P.A.I.N.

Has the prospect recognized and admitted that he has P.A.I.N. that needs to be addressed?

What are the reasons for the P.A.I.N.?

How do you know he is committed to fix his P.A.I.N.?

Have you, as the salesperson brought the prospect up the P.A.I.N. pyramid so that he/she recognizes the impact of the P.A.I.N.?

Has the person with whom you are dealing admitted the organizational impact of his P.A.I.N.?

Has the prospect recognized and admitted the personal impact of the P.A.I.N.?

Do you, the salesperson, know how much the P.A.I.N. is costing in dollars and cents?

How long has the prospect had the P.A.I.N.?

Is the prospect committed to fixing the P.A.I.N.?

Investment

Have you had a serious discussion about the price of your service?

Does the prospect have the money needed?

If they don't have money in their budget, have you with your prospect, determined how the project will be funded?

Who's budget is this solution going to impact?

Is the prospect willing to invest in a solution?

Is it going to be necessary to introduce your product in phases?

Have you had a "meeting of the minds" on the price of your product?

Does the cost of your solution make sense when compared to the cost of their P.A.I.N.?

What is the agreed-upon investment?

Who has agreed to the investment?

Is there anyone else with whom you should talk to about investment prior to Proof Presentation?

Decision

Have you talked to all the decision makers?

Who is the ultimate decision maker?

Have you been able to determine each decision maker's personal P.A.I.N.?

Do you know by which criteria they will base their decision?

Who are your supporters?

Who are your adversaries?

Have you been able to neutralize your adversaries?

What is the time frame by which a decision will be made?

Vision of Solution

Have you been able to help the prospect create his vision of an ideal solution?

Have you been able to create preference for your product and your company?

Are you able to provide the ideal solution for your prospect?

Will you be able to satisfy all of the decision makers in creating an ideal solution that will satisfy all the players?

The Importance of Debriefing

The time you spend debriefing yourself is time well spent.

You should also be asking yourself what "curve balls"

could be thrown at you. Play out possible worst-case

scenarios. What might the objections or challenges be?

How will you succinctly respond to them? The goal of

debriefing is to help you not only become keenly aware of

the information that you do have, but the information you

do not have as well.

Power Principle:
It's not what you know; it's what you don't know that will kill your sale.

Debriefing yourself should prepare you for any eventuality

you may encounter during your **Proof Presentation.**

Proof Presentations

Before implementing your solution, the typical prospect will expect to see a proposal, demonstration, references, or a walk-through, etc, that proves you can meet his expectations and solve his P.A.I.N. This step in the selling process is designed to help you effectively deliver that proof (proposal) in a way that insures a successful consummation of the sale.

What is a proof presentation? This question is asked of participants in a variety of corporate training initiatives. It is surprising to discover that there is not a uniform definition of the term. Indeed, we find that almost everyone queried has his or her own interpretation of a Proof Presentation.

What A Proof Presentation Is Not

It is not…

- A way to get the sale (if you've implemented the process correctly, you already have the sale)

- Guesswork (no guessing or assumptions)

- A means to introduce your product's Features and Advantages (focus only on what's important)

- A way to haggle over price (you have already agreed upon a price)

- A show of your expertise (they should already know)

What a Proof Presentation Is

A Proof Presentation is documentation of all the mutual agreements you have made with your prospect, either in writing or orally. There should be nothing included in the proposal that has not already been discussed and agreed upon mutually. NO SURPRISES.

When you've reached this point in the sales process, your prospect's willingness to move with you is the best indication of a successful outcome. Refer back to the qualification hierarchy, there's little left to chance. Vision of Solution has told you how the prospect will evaluate what you proposed. Assuming that you have capably shown that you meet those criteria, you can and will win the business.

Clear Next Step

Prior to delivery of your presentation (proposal), you absolutely must have a commitment about what happens next. Prior to your proposal meeting you must ask, "Let's assume that we present our solutions to you and you are convinced that we can effectively address your… (P.A.I.N.)? What would happen at that point?"

There is only one acceptable answer that would move you forward and you must get this agreement before you deliver. They must agree to make a decision. They must agree to give you a yes or no decision pending a successful presentation. NOTE: You are not pushing for the order; you are pushing for a decision.

If they agree to a yes or no decision, then schedule your presentation meeting. However, before you begin, remind them of their agreement with you to give you a yes or no decision, either of which is OK. Make certain that they are still willing to do so. Begin the meeting with a statement similar to, "We agreed that if we presented to you today, you would tell us yes we're ready to move forward and begin implementation or, no we've decided not to move forward. Is there any reason that you would not be in a position to do that today?" If they agree, proceed. If they do not agree, for whatever reason, STOP. Resolve whatever issues have caused this turnaround in their willingness to make a decision.

Another point. Unless ALL of the decision-makers are in the room, do not proceed. You will not get the order. Re-schedule your presentation at such a time that everyone who must be in attendance will be there. If you proceed anyway you might never get a chance to meet with or speak to that final person who could be the critical factor in achieving success. Do not be a victim of this stalling tactic. If it is an unfortunate situation that caused the other's absence, they should be willing to re-schedule. If it is a delaying tactic, you just gained a significant piece of information.

Power Principles:
No presentations, proposals or demo should be delivered or initiated until you know specifically what happens after they are completed.

A Word About References

Some people will ask you for references. They want to talk to others who have successfully implemented a program with you or your company. While it's tempting to provide that list with the expectation that the prospect is seriously considering working with you, history has demonstrated that that is not always true. Giving references prematurely or to unqualified prospects will diminish your chances of getting a sale.

Often the request for references is a stall or delaying tactic. Many times that request will come early in the selling process. What we have discovered is that, in reality, it will slow you and the prospect down considerably. Let's investigate why.

It is important to understand why the prospect is asking for references. However, merely asking, "Why do you need them?" is far too harsh. It is confrontational and challenging. On the other hand, asking "Do you mind if I ask you what are you hoping to hear or needing to hear from references that might help you make a better decision?" will get you some of the real reasons motivating the request. Many times you will hear P.A.I.N.

References are meaningless if the prospect:

- Has NO P.A.I.N.

- Is NOT a decision maker

- Has NO budget for your solution

- Is NOT committed to fixing his P.A.I.N.

Don't be lulled into believing that something a reference says will sell the deal. It usually will not. References are only effective in helping reassure a prospect that he is making a sound decision, not in getting the sales process started.

Therefore, when a prospect asks for references, suggest that you would be willing to share several with him at the appropriate time. Ask him if it would make sense, before he invests his time checking references, if it wouldn't be more productive to:

- Investigate his specific needs first (P.A.I.N.)

- Determine specific solutions that might be appropriate

- Determine a budget

Once this has been accomplished, you will be able to do a better job of providing him with the "correct" references that will more accurately provide him with meaningful input.

Think back to the times in the past when you have provided references. If your experience is like the majority of others who have done so, what typically happens is that the prospect takes weeks and often months before he gets around to checking them. There's no urgency. It winds up being an activity without a deadline and the prospect usually "just hasn't gotten around to it yet." You completely lose control of your selling process.

When you think about this whole business of reference checking, it's merely a way of covering oneself. The thought that you would give someone a "bad" reference is ludicrous. However, some people who are risk intolerant need reassurance and this is how they get it.

Another effective strategy in dealing with a person's need to check references is to delay it until the last step. See if your prospect will agree to that and then make the yes or no decision based upon his successfully checking references. If he agrees, be certain that you are present for the reference calls and agree on what happens after they are made, assuming he hears what he needs to hear.

Often, what you will discover if you adopt this strategy is that the need for references diminishes as you move through the Discovery Selling® process. The need for references may or may not be legitimate. By moving that to the last step, you'll effectively be able to test how necessary they really are to successfully complete the sale.

A Final Word About Proof Presentations

Delivering a Proof Presentation requires mastering the art of eliminating the extraneous. Indeed, less is better. Check the average salesperson's presentation and you'll typically find it laden with loads of unnecessary information and hyperbole. Nothing more than a formalized approach to guessing.

Your clarity in delivering the specifics your prospect needs to develop conviction and make a decision is all your Proof Presentation needs for success. Leave everything else out no matter how much you think it is really a bell or whistle they should care about. If they didn't say they wanted it, didn't say it was important, or it hadn't been discussed previously; resist the temptation to include it. You can explain all about it after you have the order. NO SURPRISES!

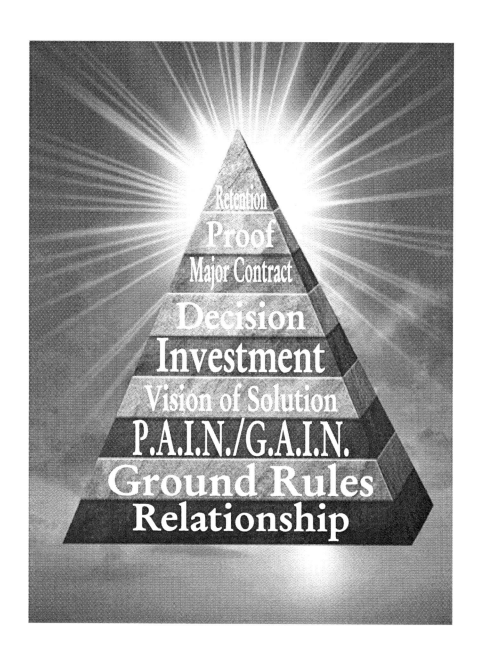

Retention

Congratulations, you have won the business! By executing the Discovery Selling® process, you now have a new customer. Is the selling over? It is not over by any stretch of the imagination. Now is **not** the time to relax. Indeed, it is now time to build a customer satisfaction strategy that will help you not just meet your customer's expectations, but exceed them. More importantly, you want to keep this customer for life. Let's look at how to accomplish this.

If you'll remember our power principle, No Surprises and No Guessing, let's take all of the ifs and maybe's out of customer satisfaction by knowing specifically what expectations must be met. You no doubt recall from the Seven Phases of Buying that the last phase is Measurement.

Once your solution is adopted and implemented, the customer will begin measuring his satisfaction level.

Exercise:

Take a moment and make a list of the possible ways that a customer might measure the salesperson and the company he has selected to supply his needs.

_____

_____

_____

_____

_____

_____

_____

- Can you measure up to all of your customer's expectations?

- Is there anything he might expect that could be difficult for you to deliver?

- What, if anything could go wrong?

- How often would he like to see you for follow up?

- How would he like to see a problem handled if one should arise?

- What would cause you to lose this business?

As you can see, these might or might not be areas that were covered when you built the Vision of Solution with your prospect. If you think you know the answers to the above questions, go the added distance to confirm that you do and that you have it right. Also make certain that nothing has changed and that the criteria which has been detailed previously is still valid. The most important thing to remember is that all of these questions must be answered if you seek to perform at a higher than expected level. Once again, to find out, you must use your questioning skills to hone in on the key information that will give you the leverage you need to keep this customer and to keep her happy.

Measurements will be either objective (measurable such as on time deliveries of supplies) or subjective (based on impressions and feeling such as there seem to be some complaints about the new pads). The subjective criteria are the hardest to understand and satisfy, because unless you know how the feelings and impressions are being measured, you won't know how to satisfy them.

Exercise:

List below, some of the objective measurements customers use to measure satisfaction.

_____

_____

_____

_____

_____

List below some of the subjective or soft measurements that customers use to determine satisfaction.

_____

_____

_____

_____

_____

Remember, you sold a solution, not a product. Is it truly solving the customer's problem? If it is not, or he doesn't think it is, you could be in trouble rather quickly.

As important as it is to know what it takes to keep the business, it is also critical to know what might cause you to lose the business. Not one in a thousand salespeople ever ask and the consequence is that they lose the business by being caught unaware. If you get blindsided and lose the business, it's your fault.

Exercise:

List below all of the reasons that you can think of that might cause a customer to stop doing business with you.

_____

_____

_____

_____

_____

_____

Seeking Complaints

You must seek complaints. That's right, you must encourage your customer to complain if he is not happy, if something is wrong or he is dissatisfied in some way. Crazy, you say? Not quite.

What would happen if, by chance, your biggest competitor just happened to prospect your "dissatisfied" customer? In the process, he suggests some reasons that they're better than you, and two of those reasons are directly related to his dissatisfaction. Any guess what happens now? Here's what research from the U. S. Office of Consumer affairs shows:

- For every unsatisfied customer who complains, there are 26 other unhappy customers who will say nothing. Of those 26, 24 of them will quit doing business with you and never come back.

- The average customer who experiences a problem with an organization will tell between 9 and 10 other people about it.

- Of the customers who register a complaint, upwards of 70 percent of them will do business with you again if their complaints are resolved to their satisfaction. That number rises to a whopping 95% if customers feel that the complaint was resolved quickly.

- U. S. businesses lose almost half of their customers every five years.

Clearly, without knowing that a complaint exists puts you in an extremely compromising position. A customer's reluctance to share complaints with a salesperson or customer service representative may arise out of the typical person's defensiveness when they hear one.

Consider a complaint as a gift from a customer. Seek to determine how the situation developed, what happened, why it happened, and when it happened. What does the customer want you to do to help? How would he like to see it resolved to make him satisfied? The number one rule is to LISTEN, LISTEN, LISTEN! Ask the appropriate questions and shut up. This is not about who is right or wrong, this is about understanding.

Encourage customers to let you know "if the ball has been dropped", if something is not right or if she believes that she is receiving poor service. Let her know that you're human and that the people in your organization are human.

> *"Betty, we work hard to keep our customers satisfied and exceed their expectations, but we're only human. We don't make many mistakes, but unfortunately we do make them. I want you to feel comfortable calling me any time if we slip up. You have my personal commitment that I will get it handled as quickly as possible and to your satisfaction. Will you do that?"*

Does this mean you cannot say "no" to a customer if she is being unreasonable in her desired resolution of a problem? Absolutely not. But, do not let her push you into an emotional mindset. Remember that when a mistake has been made, "the ball dropped", the customer will be somewhere between feeling depressed and hostile. The first thing to do is to get her calmed down. You don't do that by arguing and deflecting responsibility. You do that by listening. The person needs to vent and you are going to be the "ventee". Nothing personal, it just goes with the turf. Just listen and repeat, "I understand."

When the person finally cools down, you are going to hit her with a powerful and unexpected response. You are going to overstate the person's position by saying something like:

> *"Betty, it sounds like you'll never give us a second chance. You're very angry. I don't blame you. I would be too. This is horrible. We've let you down and I know it. Sounds like it's over for us."*

We can hear you now resisting this response, much as each of us did when we originally heard it. But think for a moment what might happen as a result of the salesperson saying this. First, the customer will usually tell you that it is NOT over. She will then tell you what she expects. That isn't bad is it? Second, the customer could agree with you and tell you that it is over. That's bad, but at least you aren't blindsided, left thinking everything is fine when it is not. Third, the customer agrees that it is over, and then gives you a chance to resurrect yourself (in effect getting back on track). She has had her chance to scold you, in essence shape you up through her Critical Parent, and now gives you another chance.

We've seen this strategy work countless times. The most crucial part is your tonality. Keep your voice soft and low and talk slowly. Mirror and match your customer, and you will be shocked at how effectively this works to defuse a heated situation.

The Annual Review

Once a year, more often if you believe it necessary, treat every customer like a prospect. Why? Because things change. New problems and new people can cause a great customer to go away fast.

Adopt the strategy that you will find and attack your weak points. Determine what new issues (P.A.I.N.) might have arisen in this customer's facility. Seek to learn the names of new people and any dissatisfactions or problems they might have had with your solutions and service. Stay close to your customer. If you do, you leave your competitors virtually no way in.

There Are No Social Calls

It's surprising to see sales call reports that state "Service Call" as a call objective. What does that mean? It is anyone's guess, and that's the problem. In sales, every call is a sales call. Service Call, unfortunately, means "Social Call" in the majority of cases. The problem is that in sales, there are _no social calls_. Therefore, no call should be made or even planned unless it can be defined as to its purpose.

That purpose is a specific call objective that can be measured.

Personal follow up visits to customers are important, but must be more than just letting them see you. Perhaps one objective is to seek problems. Therefore, no calls without a specific objective.

Defining Service

Define service. Who will you see? Why are you seeing them? How will you measure the success or failure of the interaction? These are all questions that should be asked, and answered regarding any call. So, have a valid, measurable objective on calls after the sale has been made. All customer retention calls should enhance relationship (tough to measure), find new problems and enhance the customer's business through the use of your solutions.